D1106674

The Money-Go-Round

The

MONEY

·GO·

ROUND

Lawrence A. Krause

Consolidated Capital Communications Group
Emeryville, CA • 1985

Published by Consolidated Capital Communications Group, Inc., 2000 Powell Street, Emeryville, CA 94608

Book Design by David Charlsen
Jacket Design by Communications Group Design

Manufactured in the United States of America

10 9 8 7 6 5 4 3 2 1

Library of Congress Cataloging in Publication Data

Krause, Lawrence A., 1940-
    The Money-Go-Round.

    1. Finance, Personal. I. Title.
HG179.K66   1985   332.024   85-71634
ISBN 0-930032-08-X

Distributed to the book trade by Simon & Schuster, Inc.
S&S ISBN 0-671-54869-7

CONTENTS

DEDICATION

This book is dedicated to the memory of my father, Leo Krause, who imbued me with a sense of creativity and taught me common sense . . . a most unique combination. But then, he was a most unique man.

ACKNOWLEDGMENTS

To adequately recognize and thank all those who provided assistance and encouragement during the writing of this book would be a difficult task. But to those special people who clearly influenced my thinking or provided me with substantial encouragement and technical assistance, I offer my sincere gratitude.

Art Garcia, a professional writer as well as a good friend, suggested the name of my firm and introduced me to *California Business* magazine. He also gave me substantial portions of his scarce time when I first attempted to write this book. I owe much to Art.

California Business magazine, America's largest regional business magazine, and Mike Harris, its editor, offered me the opportunity (more than six years ago) to write a monthly column. That experience provided the opportunity to hone my writing skills, and the columns became the foundation on which this book is based.

Nancy Woods, professional writer who, while knowing little about financial planning, nonetheless spent many hours acting as a sounding board and providing truly valuable advice in the writing of this book.

Richard Wollack, co-president of Consolidated Capital, offered the suggestion that I base my book on some of my columns. Without Dick, you probably would not be reading this book today.

James Miller, editor-in-chief of Consolidated Capital Communications Group, has been a source of encouragement and guidance throughout. One word best describes him ... quality.

David Charlsen is owed the credit for this creative book design. He is another professional who took his commitment seriously.

Chris Goodrich, a professional writer and my editor, evaluated and offered constructive criticism in the course of reviewing my manuscript (over and over again). I don't believe a writer could have a better editor. He is a consummate professional.

Without Kim Habenicht my thoughts would never have reached paper in a legible form. More than once she had to soak her fingers after long, long hours of typing on the word processor. She deserves the purple hand award.

George Argyris, a San Francisco attorney specializing in estate planning, reviewed the estate planning section and generously offered valuable comments — including the advice that you should see an attorney *before* you see anyone else.

Loren Dunton, founder of the International Association for Financial Planning, the College of Financial Planning, *The Financial Planner* magazine, and the National Center for Financial Education, is a highly creative individual committed to financial planning. Just being around Loren generated an awareness about people and their needs I might never have known.

Carol Wright, my business partner and good friend for almost ten years, has worked so closely with me that I'm not sure if it was she or I who wrote this book. Carol has been an enormous help in providing technical expertise as well as ideas.

Many acknowledgments conclude with such words as, "and special thanks go to my wife. . . ." More than "special thanks" are deserved by my wife Donna for her patience and understanding during the preparation of this text. A strong, loving, and supportive person, Donna helped as a sounding board for my ideas and provided me the time and encouragement to complete this book — sacrificing the needed time required to work on her master's thesis.

And finally, I know that Alexis and Danielle, ages four and nine, would have preferred their Daddy to play with them rather than be cooped up "working on his book again." Most of the time, Daddy would have preferred the same. Now our reward is that we can once again enjoy those precious moments together.

The Money-Go-Round

• Introduction

IGUANAS AND MONEY
or
How to Sleep at Night

by Shelley Berman

Have you ever gotten out of bed in the morning, looked at yourself in the mirror, turned, and asked Debbie if you were turning into an iguana? And she said yes? And you noticed she was looking a bit like an iguana herself? Read up on your zoology. Ask any herpetologist. Be very kind to iguanas because they were all once people with insomnia, just like you.

Have you ever been totally convinced that if the raw energy boiling in your upper digestive tract could be harnessed you could power the entire city of Detroit for at least two weeks? Are you aware that indigestion is not the norm but the exception — there are people in this world who do not have it — and you might just be the only antacid junkie on your block?

What is wrong here? You've always been a pretty decent person. You've just had your annual checkup and passed with flying colors. Chest, heart, blood pressure, cholesterol — A-OK! You'd take Debbie out and celebrate if the two of you weren't feeling so punk lately. Could it be you need a second opinion? Another doctor? What kind of doctor? A specialist? What kind of specialist?

Remember last week? The middle of the night? Well, what kind of specialist is needed for a person who wakes up in the middle of the night screaming, "The sky is falling! The sky is falling!" A psychiatrist? Maybe. Maybe not. Feel like talking about it?

1

There's this lot next to the house, going for a song. Beautiful piece of corner property, got to triple in value in the next year. Debbie likes it as much as I do. We might even want to keep it. A fine expanse that makes the house look so much richer. Maybe grow roses on it, or maybe a little vegetable garden. I've always wanted that. Hey, maybe even a putting green! All I know is Debbie and I would like to have it. The thing is, Aspen. We've been waiting eight years now and there's this perfect little condo up there — just great — and we love to ski, and we're not getting any younger, and we're just about ready to close on it. For pete's sake! I've been earning very well for many years now. Does it really have to be either one or the other?

I can't believe that kid. I swear, I can't believe Henry. Out of nowhere he decides to switch from law to marine biology. What a switch! A kid I had to get down on my knees and beg to throw away his water wings when he was 12 years old! Suddenly he's into marine biology. So, besides that horrendous tuition hitting me again this year, he's going to need some kind of super wet suit and scuba gear and "this fantastic new underwater camera with special lenses and, oh yes, the weirdest thing happened with the car's transmission yesterday."

I keep telling Debbie it's the Department of Water and Power, but I'm pretty sure it's not. I'm pretty sure it's the pipes. I swear, if our water gets any rustier, I can sell it as wood stain. Those old pipes down there are just about gone. Any minute now, one of those rotten old joints is going to go, and we're in for it — the deluge. We'll go floating down Maple Street like Noah's Ark. Me and Debbie, and Denise, and little George, and the two dogs, and that goofy parakeet who hasn't been right in the head since little George sucked him into the vacuum cleaner. Why am I doing this? Why am I putting off the inevitable? Why don't I just get that plumbing contractor on the phone and get it over with? Copper, that's why. It costs. And the city says new and replacement plumbing has to be copper. Why not? It's much more effective than that old steel. Longer lasting, much cheaper in the long run. What am I afraid of? Why am I hesitating to do what is so necessary to do? Am I afraid of spending the money? Why? What am I working for?

Oh happy, happy day! Denise got her learner's permit yesterday. I'm so happy I could kill myself. She'll be driving before I know it. INSURANCE! KILL! Do people know how much it costs to let your kid drive a car? Oh, how painful it is to be a father! INSURANCE! I'll have to teach

Denise about cars driving in front of her—that they have this alarming tendency to stop. I failed to teach that to Henry. He never did get the hang of it. I've often been tempted to take ads in the papers, or make public announcements: "When my son Henry is driving please do not stop your car for any reason whatsoever. It does not matter what city you are in or what direction you're driving, if you stop your car my son Henry will rear-end you." It's like a religion with him. He absolutely must drive as close as possible to the car in front. When he's driving it looks like mating season for automobiles. So now my Denise is going to be driving. I'll have two teeners driving and one subteener chomping at the bit. And Denise is going to be wanting her own car, of course. "What's Henry? Some kind of favorite around here?" DOWNPAYMENT! FINANCING! INTEREST! INSURANCE! How I hate it! How I need it!

I have simply got to get NEW PLUMBING! That funny smell in the dining room. Like damp wood. Debbie keeps mentioning it. Please, God, don't let it be what we both know very well it is. Please don't let me get into the crawl space under that floor and find that awful leak. Why not? What am I afraid of? I've worked to have this house. I love this house and want to keep it. What's wrong with spending a few bucks on it? Don't I have a few bucks to take care of my own house?

What kind of idiotic question is that? Why don't I know for sure whether or not I can afford to take care of this house and my family, and perhaps an emergency? I'm a businessman, for pete's sake! Is it possible I know how to run a business but not my own life? That's ridiculous! Or *is* it ridiculous?

Let's see. I'll close my eyes and picture my financial situation here: what I have, my earnings, my assets, my debts, etc... Wow! An amoeba! Formless! Flopping, spilling, floating without discernible shape; structureless, vague. I'm adrift! HELP! HELP! I'M A SENSIBLE MAN ADRIFT! I'M A MAN WHO DOESN'T KNOW WHAT HE HAS! OR *DOESN'T* HAVE! I'M OUT HERE IN DEEP WATER, UP TO MY CHIN, AND I'M TERRIFIED THAT IF I PUT MY FEET DOWN THERE'LL BE NOTHING DOWN THERE TO STAND ON! HELP!

Well, if ever a fellow had a reason for turning into an iguana, this seems to be it. Oh, of course he could take a sleeping pill, but the next morning that dining room floor would still smell like damp wood. Corroding plumbing is notoriously indifferent to Dalmane and Valium.

Henry would still be at college blowing transmissions and rear-ending cars and maybe deciding he's no longer interested in marine biology. Denise will soon be driving her own car with her own brand of headaches to deliver. The choice of condo or lot will remain a dilemma. But fortunately for this fellow, his condition need not worsen. It may in fact be curable, and the future may find him and Debbie looking much more like people than iguanas. He may, however, require the help of a specialist. Not a medical doctor, but a doctor nonetheless.

Enter Lawrence A. Krause. He is one of an elite new group of professionals — financial practitioners — who have arrived on the scene so recently that some folks — even those who may need them most — do not yet know about them. Mr. Krause is a financial planner. His title tells quite simply what it is he does, though it may be more correct to say that he helps people see the need for doing their own financial planning and shows them how to do it. His expertise lies in taking the mystery and fear out of what you are able to do with your money. He helps you see for yourself, without baffling and overlapping complexities — and often, hellish worry — what you have, what you don't have, what you can spend, what you can't spend, *how to plan it all out*. At the same time Krause takes into consideration the critical ingredient of change: that is, "What you have" is not the same as "What you will have" or "What you can have." He helps you plan in detail. Nothing is left out. One of this book's parts, for example, is entitled "The Predictable and the Unpredictable."

As Krause so neatly puts it, "Most people don't plan to fail. They just fail to plan."

A master of common sense and wit, Krause helps the readers take stock of themselves, quite literally, and prepare for the future while enjoying today. The emphasis here is not on money but on life — what money can and must do for our lives. It is painless reading; for all their no-nonsense talk, the pages are studded with warm humor. A bit of a hard-nosed realist, Krause does not omit the less pleasant aspects of life. This is, after all, a book about life's needs. Yet how bad can an author be if he is able to make us chuckle as he reminds us about death?

Who am I to be writing about such things? What do I know about financial planning? Absolutely nothing. And this makes me eminently qualified to speak of it. I, it so happens, am a person who did not think financial planning was necessary. I thought a fine income was all one needed. I was sure that as long as I was making money, it would all somehow take care of itself. My future was a sure thing, and I would live happily ever after. Well, today part of my income is derived from being a speaker at conferences of various financially oriented groups. My subject is entitled "Going Broke Is No Laughing Matter." I speak frankly of my personal bout with financial ruin and bankruptcy. I, who was a highly successful comedian in the late fifties and sixties, making virtually millions, was flat broke in 1979. And it wasn't due to bad luck. It was due to bad planning, or, more precisely, no planning at all, though I had a personal manager, a business manager, a lawyer, all the planners I needed. Or so I thought. Financial planning is an idea all to itself. It is its own unique practice. What I needed in those halcyon days was a specialist like Lawrence Krause.

Today, I am proud to say, Larry is my friend. He is a confidante and has been of enormous help to me in my return to solvency and peace of mind. I still don't always understand everything he says, but that's mostly because I'm a bad listener. That is a major flaw with me. If learning a few simple dollars-and-cents principles is too boring or worrying to bother with, then why not overcome the desire to have that fishing cabin or that Porsche? But that cabin and that car are very much ours to have, and the price for such possessions may not be the money so much as the institution of a sensible plan.

Let us return to our friends the Iguanas. As you read the book you will find another couple very much like the Iguanas. They are in the chapter subheaded "Getting Started," and they are John and Julia Brown. (Krause may be a very original man but not when it comes to creating character names.) Setting your goals? Now? With your children almost grown? Isn't it a bit late for goal setting? Not at all. Though Krause does note that things could have been even better if the Browns had begun their planning earlier, by no stretch of the imagination does he suggest that there is a time-limit in life for setting goals.

In a way Mr. Iguana seems to have taken the first step in getting a good night's sleep without a pill. He pictured his financial situation and recognized he was adrift. The next thing he did was yell, "Help!" Heaven knows when he has uttered an expression more apropos.

HELP! HELP! INSURANCE! LOT! CONDO! ADRIFT! FLOOD!

What's the matter, Big George? Why are you screaming?

DRIFTING! PLUMBING! CAN'T FEEL THE BOTTOM! NO SAND!

Sand? In bed? What sand? Why are you screaming?

Oh, Debbie. Oh boy. Are you awake?

Of course I'm awake. Do you think I always looked like an iguana? I'm awake almost all the time. Do you know I think we've got a plumbing leak in the dining room? There's a funny smell, like . . .

I know. But that's no reason to stay awake, Debbie.

Of course not. I'm awake because I don't want to miss the phone call.

What phone call?

The one from Henry.

Was Henry supposed to call tonight?

No, but he's about due, isn't he? I mean, it's almost two weeks now since he had his last rear-ender. I wish he'd get it over with and call. It's beginning to make me nervous. I'm beginning to worry that something may have happened to him.

Don't be silly. He's all right. Remember last year? He went for almost two months without a rear-ender.

It was summer. He was not in school. And he had a broken leg.

Try to get some sleep. I'll wake you if he calls.

Should we buy the lot, or should we buy the condo?

Maybe neither. Or maybe both. See this book? I thumbed through it. It's got some good ideas. And there's a couple in there that reminds me of us. The Browns. Some unoriginal name, huh?

I'll try to sleep. Listen, Big George. You know I don't like to complain. But you always used to call me sweet little kitten when you kissed me goodnight. Tonight you called me your cute little lizard. I prefer kitten. Okay?

Okay, Debbie. You're my sweet little kitten.

Shall I tell you a secret? I wasn't awake. I was sleeping. I mean I was actually sleeping when you started screaming.

That's wonderful. What did you take?

Nothing. You know that book you said you were going to read tonight. I read some of it myself. And I fell asleep.

Boring book, huh?

Not exactly. I was just sitting there, reading, and suddenly I was picturing beautiful copper plumbing under the house, and suddenly I was dreaming I was skiing on the lot next door.

Good night, my dear little kitten.

Good night, Big George.

HOW YOU GOT ON
THE MONEY-GO-ROUND

You've picked up this book because you're in search of financial freedom. All you really want money for is to be free from financial worries . . . to have financial peace of mind. You want to be free to enjoy your particular life-style without worrying about where the money is coming from to pay for it. You want to be free to be yourself, free to be happy.

You want to know your money is getting the best returns with safety, but questions run rampant: should I stay in "cash" or invest in something? What something? Are my taxes too high? Can I lower my tax bill? Should I get more insurance? Should I put more aside in my retirement plan? What retirement plan? How am I going to pay for the children's college? Will I outlive my resources? The questions are endless and, at times, anxious.

You do have money knowledge. But it is made up of contradictions. You have goals, but you've lost sight of how to achieve them. Your knowledge is at once broad and specialized. Like life, the world of money is filled with contradictions. If you need credit, you can't get it. If you are already prosperous, everybody wants to do you a favor. If you do not give to charity, you are stingy; if you do, it is for show.

Beyond all the questions and contradictions regarding money, there are those recurring routines. Have you ever realized that check writing ruins fully three days a month? You spend one day anticipating writing them, one day writing them, and one day upset because so much money has disappeared.

You are on the money-go-round. Up and down, round and round. But why? You have good earning capacity, intelligence, creativity, and realistic attitudes. Why then are you on the money-go-round? Haven't you had some of the best training money could buy? After all, from the time you were small, you've learned how to make it. You mowed lawns, or had a paper route, or babysat. Later you worked as a waiter or waitress.

Then came the formal training on how best to spend and invest your earnings. Courses in school, of course, were the answer. There was . . . economics, accounting and . . . well, your best classroom was really all around you. All you had to do was turn on the radio or TV or pick up a newspaper or magazine. During the course of the day you could, for example, gather knowledge about the stock market *and* experience a course on economics, all at once. "On Wall Street today, news of lower interest rates sent the stock market up, but then the expectation that those rates would be inflationary sent the market down, until the realization that lower rates might stimulate the sluggish economy pushed the market up, before it ultimately went down on fears that an overheated economy would lead to a reimposition of higher interest rates."

And when it came to other courses on investments, there was certainly no lack of information. As a matter of fact, part of the beauty of being alive is that total strangers are delighted to share their in-depth financial knowledge with you. The cab driver, the bank teller, the part-time real estate salesperson sitting next to you on the plane, as well as that part-time insurance salesperson, part-time actor, part-time waiter waiting on your full-time table. Then there were all those people who really do care about you, and want to share their financial wisdom: your barber, your beautician, your next-door neighbor, your golfing partner, your bridge partner, and even your ex-partner.

Not to worry. The professionals were also an enormous help. You have received impartial financial advice from your stockbroker, real estate agent, antique dealer, coin dealer, stamp dealer, card dealer, and doctor turned investor-wheeler-dealer. Right? Or were they?

Rounding out the picture, you sought out your accountant and attorney. After all, what better people to turn to for developing future tax and legal strategies to lower your tax bill? Both were very anxious to help. All you had to do was take the initiative. "Ask away," they said. "If you have specific questions dealing with the taxes you already paid, we'll be happy to answer them." Gee, thanks . . .

Fully educated, you were ready to strike out on your own. You knew the investment world was full of crossroads and temptations. But you were now trained. For one thing, you knew you could imitate the rich by investing to reduce the burden of taxes. It was simply bad luck the IRS disallowed your 4-to-1 tax deduction on the techniques of growing corn at the North Pole. And if only the price of oil had gone to $50 a barrel as it was supposed to, your letter of credit would not have been called, and you would not have had to sell other investment assets to meet that call. Oh yes, that Peruvian gold mine *was* a mistake. Nobody's perfect.

It's not that you're a bad money manager. As a matter of fact it was *you* who decided to purchase those 30-year tax-free bonds at an unbelievable 10 percent yield. All the economists had said the economy could not tolerate higher interest rates. So they were a little bit wrong. Though the bonds' market value plummeted for a while, you hung on, and today you're a hero.

Then there was that inside information that "Mrs. Smith's Custom Gasket and Peanut Butter Company" was going to be bought out at a substantial premium over current share price. Hank Jones, your neighbor, "got the word" from Mrs. Smith's second husband's son by a previous marriage (they're golfing partners). You bought as many shares as you could reasonably afford; a short-term killing guaranteed, Jones said. Well, it may still be a good long-term investment. But you'll probably sell once you get even.

On second thought, maybe you'd have been better off just leaving your money in the bank. At least you wouldn't have lost anything.

Personal finances can be confusing, to say the least. But the fault may not lie with you, struggling to keep up to date with changing personal needs, new financial products, and unpredictable economic and tax scenarios. The problem may in fact be a simple one called "lack of perspective." You have been unable to put this vast array of information into perspective because the wide variety of people who provide you with information have been unwilling or unable to help you put everything together.

As a matter of fact, sometimes people *want* to place you on the money-go-round. For example, the purpose of most investment seminars is to confuse you with partial information and thus create dependence on the speaker, not to educate you. Think about it. In order for you to learn all you really need to know, a speaker would have to cover the subject thoroughly, deeply, and objectively, and address all the individual concerns of every listener. That would take days, if not weeks, so it's not done.

But you do need that kind of attention to help you decide intelligently what is appropriate for you. You need a broad perspective or framework in which to apply these bits and pieces of information. Who, then, can provide the answer? *You* can. The purpose of this book is to give you the framework and perspective you need to cope effectively with the flood of unsolicited financial information you get each day and to make informed, confident decisions that truly benefit *you*.

The Money-Go-Round is an unorthodox approach to personal financial planning, and if you read it, you will take on a more confident attitude toward your own decision making. You will know how to plan — and will plan — from the inside out, starting by understanding your own needs and perceptions. The hardest part of arriving at financial security is knowing where to start. With *The Money-Go-Round* as your friend, you need no longer fear taking those first steps on your personal financial journey.

• PART I •

Getting Off the Money-Go-Round

Chapter 1

GETTING STARTED

As a professional financial planner, I have and do work with many clients: all types of people, but mostly people like you. Sure, some are millionaires, even multimillionaires. But a recurring theme among all clients is that having a lot of money doesn't guarantee peace of mind about personal finances. Quite the opposite. The more money you have, the less peace of mind you have, for more investment possibilities are open to you. These wider choices create more confusion and an even greater belief that you are not obtaining the best return on your money.

I sincerely want you to know that I understand your frustrations and your anxieties about money. And I want you to know that what you are currently facing is not unique. Though you are a unique individual, of course, you are not alone when it comes to being on a money-go-round. Look at the following list of the ten most common reasons people come to see me, or any financial planner. You'll probably find yourself identifying with one or more of these reasons. If not, ask your bookseller for a refund.

1. I'm paying too much tax: I don't want to pay more than I have to. (I've bought my *last* MX missile.)

2. I don't have the time to handle my personal financial situation properly. (I'm too busy being successful to make money.)

3. I'm not interested in personal financial matters. (It's boring.)

4. I don't grasp the "things" necessary to make a decision. (I don't know a lot about investments and I don't feel informed. A private study once revealed that 83 percent of the people who made more than $50,000 felt insecure when it came to making personal financial decisions.)

5. I want to become or know I am financially secure.

6.   I'm (still) spending as much as I am making. (There's always more month than income.)

7.   I feel like I should do something. I know I must make changes today just to stay in place.

8.   I'm confused by all the available investment choices and possible tax law changes. (It's getting too complicated and I don't know how to sort it all out.)

9.   Everyone is just trying to sell me something ... and I'm just trying to buy the right thing. (And I know the more intelligent someone is, the more rational the choice seems.)

10.   I want someone to tell me what to do and when to do it (and maybe even do it for me).

If none of these reasons apply to you, then you are qualified, or think you are qualified, to open a financial planning practice. Either way, I wish you luck.

But if you do identify with one of the above reasons, I will sum up by suggesting that we all want one thing: financial peace of mind. And since you haven't asked for a refund, you will find the rest of this book will go a long way toward providing you with just that. Time to get off the money-go-round!

Now I said I am going to help, and I am. For the first time you are going to be able to relate to your financial needs and determine what products and services will best meet those needs. I'm not going to have you fill out forms; you don't fill them out anyway. And I'll keep checklists to a minimum, even if they do make an author look good and add "bulk" to a book. Furthermore, I am not going to bore you with minutia. You are reading this book because you want to know what time it is, not how to build a watch.

In case you somehow missed my message, let me restate it. I am going to be very candid about money. This book is plain speaking, and its real entertainment value is the truth. My goal is to get you off the money-go-round by showing you not only that financial planning is not complicated, but also that it is really easy. You will be able to establish a framework within which to make the best personal financial decisions for you and your family. You will no longer believe you are somehow "missing" something important to your financial security.

Now, sit back and relax... There ... you have already taken the first step to getting off the money-go-round. And with a little practice, you will find financial planning neither intimidating nor perplexing. Believe it or not, you may already be doing a better job than you think. What's missing is confidence. You worry too much! Once you stop to think about financial decisions you're already making naturally, you can easily become confused, especially in today's changing world.

Have you ever heard the story of the ant and the centipede? The ant stopped the centipede and asked how he knew which leg he was going to move next. After all, he had *so* many. The answer was ... he never thought about it. But now that he did, for the first time he was unable to move; he couldn't figure out which leg went next. You probably have a similar problem: you think of money in terms of dollars and cents rather than what it is meant to accomplish. The old forest and trees routine.

When buying a pair of shoes it is important to determine their quality, but it is senseless to reach the point where you count the number of stitches. You are purchasing the shoes because you need them to protect your feet and would like them to complement your clothing. You will never know if you have selected the perfectly made shoe, even if you count the number of steps taken or hours worn compared to other shoes. So it is with your money. You determine its purpose, study the market, get advice, shop around a little to determine if you feel comfortable. If you do, then act. If the shoe fits, wear it.

It doesn't have to be any more complicated than that. Because in the final analysis, no one I know has ever chronicled his or her investment record to the point where he or she saw, or even felt, the return of that extra-hard-fought 1 or 2 percent achieved over a long period of time. Have you? When was the last time you placed money in a 25-year account that was unencumbered by inflation, taxes, and other investment performance — an account that continually maintained that 2 percent edge?

Usually, the time you spend playing interest rate tag would be better spent on your job or with your family. You would likely make more money and find yourself less exasperated. Life itself is a series of trade-offs, and the world of personal financial decisions is no different.

Of course, I suggest you monitor your investment performance from time to time and make adjustments when necessary. But treat your portfolio like a good pair of shoes; don't throw it out unless it no longer functions or will take too much time or money to repair.

I am asking you to step back and view your money from a different, less frightening perspective. Don't believe all you read or hear. You will often find that your current investments aren't so bad. And if you have made errors, they are not the end of the world. In all probability, all you need to do is diversify more.

Though I've asked you not to get too caught up in details, let me just ask whether you have ever thought about this detail; your attitude toward money — its emotional impact on you.

We all have such attitudes, you know. And before you can think about mapping out a financial plan, you first must think about your emotional relationship to money. Are you the type of person who must save for a rainy day? Are you a product of the Great Depression, or did your parents imbue you with a sense of the depression from their experiences that you've never quite shaken? Are you a compulsive saver, afraid to let go of your cash no matter what? Are you reluctant to reveal how much you make, how much is in the bank, or how much the house cost? Do you feel you must get rid of money? Do you know how to enjoy it or spend it? Do you experience your money as a current event rather than future purchasing power?

I have a client who is a single, 42-year-old tailor. He has squirreled away $600,000 in bank CDs and money market funds. He works seven days a week, rents his apartment, and owns few material goods. He was constantly saving money because he lived in fear that he would lose his job, might not find another, and had no one to turn to. He never knew when he might need as much cash as he could accumulate. Yet he did not have the ability to use the money constructively to better his life today.

I often see widows whose husbands previously handled the family finances. The widow lives very frugally because she is in constant fear her money will run out before she does. And I can't help but observe how often "seasoned citizens" are obsessed by the belief that serious medical costs may decimate their assets. Consequently, they tend to hoard their money as never before.

All these individuals are victims of attitude. None has taken the time to determine what their future needs might actually be. They may not change old habits when they become better informed, but their money anxiety drops. The money-go-round slows down.

Why is that important? Because until you realize what type of person you are about your money, you will *never* achieve financial peace of mind. Just recognizing that you are unable to change or don't care to will help you take the first step to lowering your money anxiety. As Thoreau once said, "That man is richest whose pleasures are the cheapest." If you conclude that your threshold is a 30-month certificate of deposit (see chapter 8) yielding 10 percent, so be it. At the moment, in fact, such a return would put you ahead of inflation. Most important, your capital would be safe. You may not get rich, but you can have peace of mind.

You might have a good laugh over a story told by one of my clients. He's in his eighties, a high achiever who hates losing, but he knows himself so well he can repeat a story of lost opportunity with good humor.

About 60 years ago, as an insurance claims agent, he paid $5,000 to a claim recipient in Lake Tahoe, California. The recipient said he was going to use the money to buy ten lakefront lots at $500 apiece.

My client considered making the same investment, but chose not to. Today he says that was one of his best financial decisions ever. Had he purchased similar lots, he says, he would probably have sold them after they had doubled or tripled in value. Now that they are worth more than $1 million apiece, he doesn't feel at all bad because he never owned them in the first place.

Like this fellow, you need to gain perspective about yourself. If you find you can't do it yourself, ask a friend of the same sex, age, and socioeconomic level to help out. Ask what he or she understands or recognizes about your financial attitudes. You will find this discussion enlightening — perhaps even exhilarating.

The next step to gaining financial perspective and peace of mind is to take your bearings and know where you stand. As in traveling, you must determine where you are before you can figure out how far you have to go and what mode of travel is best. A plane isn't a very good choice if your destination is only 15 miles away.

THE EXAMINATION

Now for a small bit of paperwork. Ask your banker or look in a financial planning guide for a net worth statement (the amount by which assets exceed liabilities) or just use a blank sheet of paper.

List what you own and what you owe. Make sure you distinguish your *personal* assets from your *investment* assets. Your home, a painting, a classic car, and a diamond ring may all be worth a lot of money, but they're no more valuable than your shoes, in monetary terms, if you do not *plan* to sell them to put food on the table. True, they can be considered investments of last resort, but if you have that great a need for cash, you probably won't get even a reasonable price for them. Personal assets should not be included in your financial plan other than to be sure they are protected from loss.

Tax refunds, cash value in your life insurance, real estate, limited partnerships, equity in your business, bank accounts, securities, bonds, trusts, retirement plans (yes, they do have a specific value at a specific point in time), money owed to you by relatives, and so on — every investment asset or debit you can think of should be counted. On that note, don't be overwhelmed by the following list. Its completeness is simply meant to remind you of possible assets or liabilities that may have slipped your mind.

Financial Summary

Investment Assets	Bank accounts; cash; certificates of deposit; term deposits; U.S. savings bonds; foreign accounts; notes receivable; mortgages receivable; stocks; options; stock options; futures; bonds; tax-deferred annuities; mutual funds; real estate and tax-sheltered investments, such as oil and gas and equipment leasing; IRAs, Keoghs, and other qualified vested retirement plan(s) or nonqualified plans; interest; deferred income; precious metals, gems, collections, and artwork; cash value in insurance policies; trusts; business interest(s); royalty interest; near-term inheritances; gifts; known future income.
	I am sure there are some investment assets I missed, so please don't assume this list is definitive. And remember if there are two of you, be sure to include both sets of assets. If you have children, create a separate list of their assets.
Liabilities	Mortgages payable; margin debt; notes payable; letters of credit outstanding; income, gift, or estate tax due; credit card debt; tuition; child support; known future expenses.

Now subtract your liabilities from your assets. The result is your net worth. Hopefully, you'll end up with a number greater than zero: that's called a positive net worth.

After determining your net worth, what does it tell you? A lot. You'll better visualize how well you're putting your money to use. You may find, for example, that the debt you've been taking on is unreasonable, and your insurance isn't keeping pace with the growing value of your property, that your emergency cash is too low for your income, or that your budgeting is poor. But a personal financial statement can do much more than indicate immediate deficiencies. By forcing you to consider your circumstances, it gets you thinking and helps you guide your financial future.

Now look at your income — paycheck, dividends, interest, profits, etc. — and expenses — everyday costs, monthly bills, alimony, child support, and so on. Compare them with figures from previous years and project them into the future 5 or 10 years, or to "old age" (which is 15 years ahead, no matter what your current age). Don't forget inflation. Assume some inflation rate and multiply these figures by that number for each year you're projecting into the future. If you are not mathematically inclined, you may need help in figuring future values. Don't forget to subtract projected taxes each year.

Are you gaining or losing ground, once taxes and inflation are taken into account? Are you expecting a significant increase or decrease in your income? Do you have more money than you need for everyday expenses? If so, do you spend it anyway, or do you save it? Could you cut unnecessary or marginal expenses in order to invest some money and thus achieve your goals?

Ask yourself, "Where do I want to be in 5 years? 10 years? Beyond that, say 20 or 30 years? What do I want to achieve in life during those periods? Do I intend to stay in the same profession or job? Will my family be larger? Do or will my children want to go to college? Am I approaching or considering an early retirement, or do I plan to retire or slow down in 20 or 25 years?" You may think it's silly to think about these events so far in advance, but then again, if you're 62 to 65 at that time, you know very well that Social Security won't meet all your needs. Be sure to determine whether your desires coincide with those of your family.

Obviously, none of these examples will apply exactly to your situation. They may not even be close. You may have little desire for material things, you may be childless, or you may have so much money that you needn't worry about retirement or education funding. But the principle is the same: planning for your future will ease your mind, and actually doing something about it is a damn *high* — regardless of your financial situation. Planning allows you to make the future a little more predictable, a little less threatening. Thinking positively about your financial future and the steps you need to take puts you in control of the future rather than the other way around.

SETTING YOUR GOALS

I know, goals are boring. But you need to get pumped up about them. If I handle this one right, much of the rest of your financial life will fall neatly into place.

Of these first few steps in financial planning, probably the most important is determining your goals. When I begin to work with a new client, we talk about this for a long time. We have a freewheeling discussion often lasting four or five hours (you can do this with your "significant other" or with friends). Usually it's only after two or three hours have passed that we get down to what the client *really* wants. That's how out of touch most of us are with our basic desires and deepest goals. They *are* there: it's just a matter of finding them. Don't stop digging until you're certain what you want from life, and be sure to include your family in the discussion.

Once you know *where* you're going, the next step is to decide *how* to get there. If you divide the future into five-year segments, you can plot a route that takes your major goals into account. Let's take an example and draw up a financial road map.

John Brown is 42 years old, his wife Julia is 40, and they have two teenage children, Kim and Matt. The family lives together in a nice house with a big mortgage, and both parents have healthy incomes. John may be transferred soon by his company, but he isn't sure when, if ever, the transfer will occur. Julia works half-time as a freelance word processor. Kim is intent on getting her driver's license and doing well in her prep school. And Matt, a budding young history buff, is dying to go to Europe. Each member of the family has different things on his or her mind, and John — who runs the household finances — must make sense of all their goals. He comes up with a sketch like this:

YEARS: **5** **10** **15** **20** **25**

Major purchase/ Children in college		Early retirement	Frequent traveling	Steady income

To John, 5 years — let alone 25 years — seems a long way off, lost in the haze of the future. But he knows this chart will act as a reminder: something for him to keep in the back of his head, to inform, if not influence, his current decisions. John wants to improve even further the quality of his planning decisions, however, so he creates a chart with a narrower focus. Having gained a sense of the big picture, John is ready to chart his more immediate goals in detail.

John wants to buy, at her urging, a used car for Kim. But he also wants to take his family on a European vacation, partly as a gift to Matt but mostly because the family has never traveled abroad together. Other large expenses are looming as well; the house needs painting, and Julia — who loves cross-country skiing, camping, fishing, and general peace and quiet — has suggested buying a mountain cabin, or a time-share with another couple. John creates another chart with these purchases in mind.

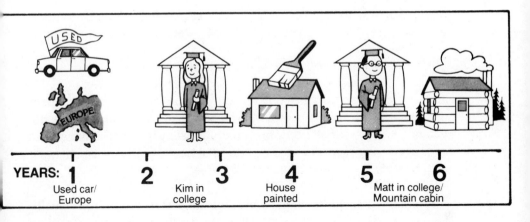

YEARS: 1	2	3	4	5	6
Used car/ Europe		Kim in college	House painted		Matt in college/ Mountain cabin

John looks at his finances, making sure that he is taking inflation, taxes, and his regular investments, which include an IRA, into account. He then asks himself, "Can I in fact afford all these things over the next five years, or should I delay some purchases? Is Kim more set on a fine college education or a used car—or can I manage both by making my money work more efficiently? Which of these things do I want *most*, which do we want *now*?" John is seeking *financial perspective*, for it is perspective that gives him control.

John also asks himself, as you will, the practical questions. If we do have to move soon, will painting the house be a good idea? Probably, but John can delay that until he knows for certain about his transfer. He also goes beyond the simple money factors. This transfer business has upset the whole family; perhaps they *need* an exciting family vacation more than anything else. When John asks his family, he finds that Julia would be just as happy going to Europe this summer as buying that time-share cabin they saw. John makes the cabin a more distant goal, with Julia's blessing.

Perhaps Kim can help out, too. Would she prefer a car now or Europe now and a car later? Or both now and two years at a state school before finishing up at a private college? Or could John get the car, take the family to Europe, and pay Kim's private school tuition, *if* she's willing to take a dining hall job at college? Can *all* these goals be achieved by placing them in the proper order and planning for each individually?

John is sorry he has to make these choices, forcing his family to compromise, but that's the result of his late start on financial planning.

Your situation, of course, will be different from John's, but your analysis will be similar. Each of your goals will likewise entail a different kind of planning, and that's one reason why the most important aspect of a financial plan is its *balance*. No ready-made plan can achieve the balance you personally require: what you want is a plan that reflects *your* needs and resources over a period of time. For that reason it must also be able to evolve; it must be *flexible*.

A balanced, flexible financial plan allows you to accumulate wealth for tomorrow without sacrificing the money you need today. You must be patient, however, in accumulating that wealth; like everyone else, we must crawl before we walk and walk before we run. By investing wisely, you'll eventually get to the point where you needn't delay needed purchases in order to assure your future. In fact, you may well find that once you know your financial abilities and limitations, you'll only want those things that lie within your extended grasp. You'll soon be living up to your greatest financial potential.

In the meantime, be a little realistic. Go ahead and dream about Ferraris, but don't confuse dreams with reality; if you suddenly did get that kind of money, would you be better off buying a car immediately, or investing the money while you thought more about the purchase? An expensive sports car will put you in the fast lane, no doubt about that. But remember the story of the tortoise and the hare? Once you've thought about it, you might prefer a Volkswagen tortoise to a Ferrari hare (after all, your tortoise could be a Rabbit). The money you invested instead of spending will soon provide you with money (perhaps including Ferrari money) for all your life goals. No matter what you decide, you'll have made a conscious choice.

As your personal financial plan matures, you'll develop a portfolio for all seasons. You'll have sufficient liquidity for cash needs, emergencies, and unexpected opportunities and investments targeted for your future and that of your children. You'll have the flexibility, too, to respond to changes in the money system, and you will no longer have to worry whether the economy or the income tax rules are going to zig or zag. Come inflation, recession, or depression, you'll be prepared because your various investments carry income, growth, and hedges against disaster.

An impossible dream? Not after your financial plan framework is in place. Once you've defined your goals, you've broken through the anxiety barrier, and you are beginning to take control. Just keep in mind that your *goals* are more important than your money.

• PART II •

The Predictable and the Unpredictable

Chapter 2

ESTATE AND EDUCATION PLANNING

ESTATE PLANNING

An excellent trivia question might be, "There is only one event that is simultaneously predictable and unpredictable. What is that event? Answer: Death." Death is predictable because not even taxes are that sure and unpredictable because no one ever knows just when the event will take place . . . unless a firing squad is about to receive its orders. I like to refer to the event as "an untimely death," for when is death timely? As a practical matter, all future financial planning is worthless unless estate planning is included, for without it you will undo much of the legacy that most of us spend a lifetime trying to accumulate. That is why I am addressing the issue of estate planning early in the book. You will either lose much of your estate to taxes (now your heirs can watch your estate purchase more MX missiles) or create many unnecessary problems for others. Either can happen through improperly directed assets, extensive and expensive delays, high legal costs, or other complications, such as court-appointed guardians for your children.

Estate planning does not have to be any more difficult than preparing a simple will. And if any single element calls for immediate attention, it is the lack of an up-to-date will. Time required — about an hour. Expenses involved — from $10 to maybe $250 or $350. Yet, it has been estimated that more than 70 percent of Americans die without any kind of will.

The cost of hiring a lawyer to prepare a will isn't the problem, nor is the time involved. The problem is that no one likes to think about, talk about, or do anything about his or her inevitable death. But you must, even if it's just this once.

Those of you who say "I don't need a will" usually base the statement on one or more of the following assumptions:

1. You don't have enough assets to bother.

2. You are single.

3. Your spouse will automatically get everything.

4. All of your more substantial possessions are jointly held, providing for immediate ownership by the surviving spouse.

All four assumptions could easily be wrong.

Not enough assets to bother? Now that you have compiled an investment financial summary, add to it all your personal assets: personal things such as your auto(s), boat(s), plane(s), recreational vehicle(s), collection(s), jewelry, antiques, clothing, and your home and/or vacation home, unless you were planning to sell them and use the proceeds as an investment asset. Once you add the proceeds from your life insurance policies (don't forget company-paid policies) and pension/retirement death benefits to your estate, you will know the extent of your total worth. Surprising, isn't it?

The excuse of being single is a cop-out. I'll bet you don't know for sure where your state says your assets must go if you don't specify your intent. I'll also wager that if you're living with someone, you don't really wish him or her left out. And have you any idea how long it can take for an estate to be settled? And what about the chance you'll become unable to take care of yourself due to an accident, stroke, or senility? Simply seeing an attorney or financial planner for a will might set you on the road to obtaining a living trust (a living will) whereby someone could step in to help you without having to have you declared incompetent. I can go on, but I hope you get the point.

The third assumption, that the surviving spouse will get everything, is most unlikely. When you die without a will, the rigid descent and distribution laws of your state take over. In most states where there is no will, a will would be drawn on your behalf, which might look like this:

Being of sound mind and memory, I, John Brown (also known as Mr. Iguana), do hereby publish this as my last will and testament:

First, I give my spouse only one-third of my possessions, and I give my children the remaining two-thirds.

A) I appoint my spouse as guardian of my children, but require that she report to the probate court every year to account for her expenses in caring for our children.

B) I direct my spouse to put up a performance bond so the probate court will have a guarantee that she will exercise proper judgment in handling, investing, and spending our children's money.

C) I give my children the right, as soon as they reach legal age, to spend their inheritance as they see fit and to demand and receive a complete accounting from their mother of all her financial actions with their money during their minority.

Second, should my wife remarry, her husband shall be entitled upon her death to one-third of everything she possesses, including what she inherited from me. The second husband shall not be bound to share any of this portion with my children, regardless of age, should they need additional support.

Third, should my spouse predecease me or die while any of my children are minors, I do not wish to exercise my right to nominate their guardian. Should my relatives and friends be unable to select a guardian by mutual agreement, I direct the probate court to make the selection. If the court wishes, it may appoint a person completely unknown to me as guardian.

Fourth, since I prefer to have my money spent by the government rather than used for the benefit of my wife and children, I direct that no effort be made to lower the taxes incurred at my death.

A court-appointed administrator is frequently faced with the need to secure a bond equal to or greater than the value of the estate. The bond and the step-by-step reporting requirements of the court all cost money, considerably more money, in all likelihood, than a lawyer's fee for preparing a will. In some states, the laws require that the money be set aside for minor children until the children come of age. In the meantime, the mother of those children can be in serious financial difficulties.

The fourth assumption, that joint ownership replaces the need for a will, also has its pitfalls. Should a husband and wife be in an accident and both die at the same time under circumstances that make it impossible to determine which one died first, even property held jointly can be distributed under intestacy laws. (Dying "intestate" means dying without a will.) Again, the state prevails unless there is a will. If a childless couple dies in an accident, but the wife lives only a few seconds longer than the husband, the couple's jointly held assets could end up in the hands of the wife's relatives, with nothing going to any of the husband's family. This could happen even though her nearest relative may be a distant and disliked cousin, while the husband's parents are alive and impoverished.

Maybe you need a will to put "brakes" on surviving beneficiaries so that they cannot dissipate their inheritance unwisely. Or maybe you want to determine exactly what you own and exactly what your spouse owns. Or . . .

There are as many advantages to making a will as there are disadvantages to dying without one. The basic difference is between being in control and being out of control. If you are one of those people who do not have a will and honestly know it will take more than one week before a will can be drawn by an attorney, then after you finish the next two paragraphs, please put this book down and follow these instructions.

There are do-it-yourself wills called holographic wills. Not all states recognize holographic wills, and many wills of this type have been declared invalid by the courts for technical errors that seem silly. Should your lack of knowledge about the fine points of the law, or about whether your state recognizes holographic wills, stop you from writing one? Absolutely not. Anything is better than nothing. The important thing is to make a will ... hopefully a thoughtful one.

Just take a plain piece of paper (yes, it can have lines) and, entirely in your own handwriting, state your desires clearly and succinctly. If you make a mistake or want to change something, write the page over. Date and sign the will, and that's it. No witnesses are required. Do not have it notarized, and do not make a joint holographic will. It is valid only for the person who writes and signs it.

Sure, there's more. But I'm not trying to practice law — far from it. I just want to get you started, and now you've taken an important first step. The next is to get yourself to a lawyer to do it just so.

Recently, I visited a neighbor who has five young children. When he told me he and his wife had no will, I was compelled to jump on my soapbox. Though they are warm and compassionate people, they were unintentionally and unknowingly being selfish in the extreme. It wasn't so much the money, but if something happened to both of them, what would happen to their children? Who knows? The family might even have to be split up. I had them write a holographic will then and there. About three weeks later they were able to visit an attorney and have a will professionally prepared.

If you already have a will, you probably haven't looked at it in years. That creates another problem, the obsolete testament. It was once wise, for instance, to incorporate a trust in a will, in order to reduce or eliminate federal estate taxes incurred on the death of a spouse. But laws change over the years; the Economic Recovery Tax Act of 1981 significantly limited the number of estates subject to estate taxes, making some trusts unnecessary or even counterproductive.

If your attorney has not contacted you about changing your will, take the initiative yourself.

By the way, don't forget to prepare a list of all your holdings. The most carefully drafted estate plan is worthless if your heirs can't find your assets. You might also consider writing a letter to your heirs. This could be an informal letter telling them where your important documents (will, life insurance policies, etc.) are located. Even if your spouse knows, he or she might predecease you. Also include your wishes and desires on certain nonlegal matters, such as burial requests, whom to consult about major financial decisions, how to dispose of certain properties, what income or debts are still expected, and even who gets which personal effects. Although this letter is not legally binding, clear instructions from you may help settle any disagreements.

It never ceases to amaze me that people seem to become concerned about estate planning when they are about to embark on a trip overseas. One such person — not even a client at the time — felt so strongly about planning that before he embarked on a trip to Europe he told me of a letter he had prepared for his family, telling them to contact me in the event of his demise.

In case you haven't noticed, I have hardly mentioned trusts. Trusts have been treated as the answer to every estate-planning problem.

Though it is generally possible to reduce the costs of estate administration, avoid publicity about estate assets, and soften taxes through a trust, a trust is no cure-all. There are trusts that have a great deal of flexibility and some that don't. But unless you have a will, a trust is putting the cart before the horse. Since 70, perhaps even 80, percent of you (including most attorneys) have an outdated will or none at all, why should I spend another 10 or 20 pages keeping you on a money-go-round by confusing you with an in-depth discussion about trusts? If you are interested in learning more about them, see an attorney who is an estate planning specialist, or read some of the hundred or so estate planning books, attend one of the 900 seminars, consult with one of the 200,000 insurance agents, or seek out any financial planner or bank trust officer. They will be more than happy to fill in the gaps.

If you already have or just completed an up-to-date will, you are to be commended for having faced the issue of estate planning — and you probably feel pretty good about it, too. The next step — a higher level of estate planning — might make you feel even better. But I'm not going to mislead you. You will never feel as good about your death plan as your life plan — unless you can find a way to enjoy the results after you're gone.

Furthermore, I want to be sure you're aware that the best estate planning requires the services of a lawyer. Not only because it's complicated, but because it is illegal for nonlawyers to give legal advice. That may sound unfair, but there is a reason for the restriction; our legal system is complex, difficult to understand, and constantly evolving in very subtle ways, which means that only attorneys can really keep a firm grasp on it. A good financial plan must take advantage of existing laws, and that means a good attorney (again, usually an estate specialist) is ultimately a necessity.

EDUCATION FUNDING

In addition to death and taxes (don't worry — I cover taxes in chapter 13), there is another "predictable" people often overlook: college education costs. The "pain" of pay-as-they-go college funding is unbelievable. As one of my clients said, "It's far worse than alimony." Some express it in other financial terms by saying it's like adding three teenage daughters to the family overnight.

It has often been said that after warmth, love, and a stable environment, the greatest thing parents can give their children is a quality education to prepare them for life on their own. And since each person is his or her own best investment asset (see chapter 7) education is a very wise investment in that asset. To have to deny your children the opportunity or endure a lot of pressure to meet the ongoing expense truly places you and your children on the worst of money-go-rounds. You know education expenses are imminent; the time to start setting money aside is *now*! This is not the time to say, "I'll think about it," or "I'm sure I'll be able to handle it when the time comes." By 1990, four years of tuition, fees, room, board, books, supplies, transportation, and some personal items are likely to cost more than $75,000 at a private college and more than $35,000 at a public college. I suggest you call a typical school and ask them to provide projections. They can.

There are infinite combinations and permutations of college funding strategies for your children. But first you have to determine your attitude about higher education costs and how you are going to pay them. Do you intend to pay for everything yourself, or do you plan to have your son or daughter help out? Nearly 60 percent of the students at private colleges and universities, and about 30 percent of those at public institutions, receive some form of financial assistance. Are you going to count on that assistance, or pray that your child's grandparents will come to the rescue? They may have to.

Perhaps you want to handle it yourself? If so, the most important principle to understand is that you are wasting money if you pay with after-tax dollars. There are better techniques for creating an education fund, with most techniques using the principle that education should be funded with pretax dollars.

The techniques I'll discuss below all involve income-shifting from your tax bracket to that of your child, which is undoubtedly lower. Any of these vehicles will save, or at least substantially reduce, the taxes on resources and will lead to a more cost-effective college-funding program. No expert help is needed for most of the tactics I suggest, but the first three — trusts, gifts, and no- or low-interest loans — are among the long-range options that will probably require the assistance of a lawyer, accountant, or financial planner.

Trusts

I have avoided an in-depth trust discussion up to this point, and trust me — I'm not about to overdo it now. But you must at least be aware of some of the following trust techniques in order to be able to ask better questions of an advisor. And who knows, you might even be able to come to some conclusions right now about what works for you.

You can shift income to your child's lower tax bracket by establishing a reversionary trust, also known as a Clifford, ten-year, or grantor trust. Here, income-producing assets are placed in the trust for a minimum of ten years and a day. After that, the assets revert to the donor, and the income is distributed to your child (as long as it is not used for his or her "support," which does not include college expenses). This trust allows everyone to benefit; it provides your child with a higher education at a low real cost to you. And you don't lose an asset that may be important for your own future security, since it reverts to you.

Though you've probably already heard or read about this educational-funding method, you're not likely to use it. In the past 15 years

I've known only eight people who have used this type of trust: most people either don't have the right kind of an asset for a Clifford trust, or it seems too expensive to set up, or too "complicated." It makes nice reading, but it probably won't apply to most of you. Besides, future legislation may change the effectiveness of this trust.

Minor's Trust

The minor's trust allows you to pass on your assets to your child when he or she turns 21 and not before, even though the age of maturity in most states is 18. The principal and income may be used for the child's benefit before the age of 21, then it becomes the child's property. The income tax advantage, once again, is derived from income shifting, the trust is likely to be accumulating income at a lower tax rate.

The income can be accumulated until needed for college expenses, and then both income and principal can be used to pay for those expenses. As was the case with the Clifford trust, the assets will be under the management and control of the trustee. And similarly — due to the expense of establishing this trust, along with accounting fees and other complexities — it will not be useful to very many of you. So don't be overly concerned about learning all the details. If it does seem as though it might be appropriate, however, see your attorney.

Gifts

Who ever said 'tis easier to give than to pay with after-tax dollars must have been thinking about college education costs. Financial gifts are another alternative that can benefit both sides, and this is the easiest one to do. A parent can give a tax-free gift of up to $10,000 in cash or liquid assets (stocks, bonds, mutual funds, etc.) to each child (or to anyone) each year without incurring any federal gift tax. Two parents can give $20,000 to each child tax free. In addition, amounts paid directly to an educational institution on behalf of your child are not considered taxable gifts. Your child will not have to pay any tax on receiving the gift. You do not deduct the gift, but a sum given to your child today, growing in that lower tax bracket, will eventually be worth far more than a similar sum growing in your bracket.

Under the Uniform Gift to Minors Act (UGMA), a law adopted by most states, or the Uniform Transfers to Minors Act, adopted by some states, a gift given to a minor is fully vested, legally theirs, and recorded under the child's Social Security number. That's good for the child; what's good for the parent is that the underage child must have a custodian trustee to manage the gift until the child legally becomes an adult — and that person can be the parent. The one pitfall is that if you should die while still the custodian, the gift account will be considered part of your estate and must go through probate. The same thing could happen in your spouse's case, if he or she is considered a joint donor of the gift (as may happen in a community property state); therefore, it's best to have someone other than a donor act as custodian. In their own names, minors can receive life insurance policies on their own lives, U.S. savings bonds, and savings accounts.

Under the UGMA, gifts are economical, flexible, and simple, and they can save your family a lot of money. Let's look at an example. Assume you're in the 35 percent tax bracket, and that you have $20,000 you'd like to invest. If you invest that sum at a 10 percent interest rate, you'd end up with $37,540, after taxes, in ten years. If you give the $20,000 to your child, however, and invest it on his or her behalf at the same rate for the same amount of time, your son or daughter would end up with $51,619, or 38 percent more than what you would have earned yourself. The difference is money that would have evaporated in taxes.

Giving gifts to your child can help you out in other ways as well. If you have recently bought a stock or property that you discover doesn't fit your plans, you could avoid the short-term capital gains tax by giving that asset as a gift to your child. The child would assume your cost basis, and then he or she (or the guardian) could sell the asset and realize the short-term capital gain at his or her lower tax bracket.

Generally, such a strategy is most suitable for investments that have matured (outlived their original purpose) or are being considered for sale anyway. A "matured" investment might be real estate that has lost most of its depreciation tax benefits, for example, a real estate limited partnership. Another "mature" investment might be an oil and gas partnership from which you've taken all the initial deductions: now you can pass on the income stream to your children.

Giving cash to your child for college funding is a viable strategy only if it's made several years in advance. Cash given well ahead of college costs has the time to grow (if invested in growth- oriented investments such as stocks) or to compound income (like money market funds or savings). In either case, the income realized (whether ordinary or capital gains) would be taxed at the child's lower bracket. And in either case, you will not feel the "buck" of the money-go-round horse.

I should add, and emphasize, a note of caution: Gifts to your children really are gifts. You can't attach legal strings to a gift as you can with a trust, so if Kim wants to buy a Rolls Royce instead of going to college when she legally becomes an adult, she can. Parents can usually exert "parental influence," of course, but if that influence doesn't seem sufficient to you, you might be better off setting up a trust or a low-interest loan.

No- and Low-Interest Loans

Much has been written about the pros and cons of this income-shifting strategy. In brief, the strategy goes as follows: you lend cash to your child, or a trustee if the child is a minor, and either low or no interest is charged the child. The note is usually a "demand" or "call" loan, and the funds are invested in high-yielding assets taxable to the child in his or her low bracket.

Loans can be a reasonable compromise between trusts and gifts. You don't have to wait ten years to get your money back as you do with a Clifford trust, and unlike a gift, you *can* get your money back. A low- or no-interest loan is inexpensive to set up and allows the parents to recover the money at any time, if they stipulate payment on demand.

You should be very cautious when setting up one of these loans, however, for not only is their legal form critical but also the IRS has instituted so many new rules that much of their benefit has been diluted. For example, depending on its use, the government can impute a minimum rate of interest on the loan and/or treat it as a taxable gift (however, the gift tax annual exclusion would apply). The law regarding such loans has gotten sufficiently complicated that you must talk to your lawyer or tax advisor before considering one. If all these details about loans confuse you, or frighten you, then in all likelihood you should not consider one.

Other Strategies

There are quite a few additional strategies that can help you build an education kitty. For example, you may wish to develop a line of credit at a bank to borrow for future college expenses. You may also be able to borrow up to $50,000 from your pension plan, as long as you pay it back in five years or less. And, of course, you can borrow against the equity portion of your home. There are guaranteed student loans as well, for which the government pays all the interest until six months after graduation.

Today almost half the nation's colleges make it possible to spread tuition payments over many years. If you own a business in which your child is employed, you can consider letting the business pay your child's college expenses by establishing an educational benefit trust for your child and the children of qualified employees (like those who have worked for the company two years or longer). If the business is large, you could start a scholarship program for employees' children.

If you're really creative, you can use an IRA to fund college educations. Again, if you own your own business, you can use the new IRA laws to fund a major part of your child's college education within a four-year period. And it's all legal (though it works most efficiently if your business is incorporated).

Make sure the children you employ are doing legitimate work, and pay them a fair wage, just as you would any other employee. If your child makes, say $4,300 each year, he or she can open an IRA and put in $2,000 each year. Most of your child's remaining earnings would not be taxed because with a $4,300 annual income, the child is in the zero bracket. If the IRA earns 10 percent for four years, he or she would have in excess of $10,000, and could have another $10,000 if he or she saved working wages. All this is tax free even if your child incurs a 10-percent IRA penalty for withdrawing the money to pay for college. At the 35 percent federal bracket, you would have to earn $30,800 (a 54 percent greater amount) to accomplish the same net result.

There are additional methods that financial advisors can tell you about in greater detail. I'll describe one more in chapter 8: zero coupon bonds.

Remember what I said earlier about wills? Any will is better than no will. Well, if college costs are ahead, any shifting of income is better than no shifting; any technique is better than the nothing you are probably doing now.

• Chapter 3

RETIREMENT PLANNING AND DOING

THE PLANNING

Drawing up a will can give you a great sense of satisfaction. Unfortunately, you cannot be around to enjoy the reward ... watching your heirs get the proceeds. But with retirement planning, all the rewards are yours to enjoy.

Planning for retirement does not mean you must actually plan to retire. It simply ensures that the money you don't need now will pay good dividends when you're older: what you invest today will help replace the money you won't be earning if you want to slow down or in fact retire. Consequently, the primary goal of retirement planning is a stable, income-producing investment fund that will enable you to maintain your current standard of living.

Unfortunately, more than 70 percent of the population (60 million people 50 or older) approach retirement with no preparation. And of Americans reaching the age of 65 or older, an astonishing 62 percent have less than $6,000 annual income. Only 8 percent have incomes over $15,000 per year, including Social Security; 79 percent have assets of less than $35,000.

And don't be too sure of yourself if you think you're affluent today. A recent study from SRI International (formerly Stanford Research Institute) showed that the working person between 50 and 65 who made more than $40,000 per year had median investment assets of only $131,000. Scary, isn't it? Can you image attempting to retire on the income generated by that sum?

Fortunately, our government recognizes the need for adequate retirement planning. It also recognizes that Social Security (yes, I believe there will be a social security in the future) will not even come close to taking care of us during our later years. So it has provided tax incentives for individuals, employers, or both to encourage us all to do something more.

Clearly, more assets providing still greater sources of income are still needed, and it has to be up to us to provide them. Retirement seems very far away to many people, but the sooner you think about it, the more you can do about it.

IRA

Employee-benefits consultants and financial planners call it Congress's greatest gift in 50 years. Thanks to the Economic Recovery Tax Act of 1981, anyone who earns compensation may now open an Individual Retirement Account (IRA).

What gift could be better? Here is something that will cut your taxes. Something that will help you provide for a secure, comfortable future. Something that can even be fun. Yet so far only 35 percent of all eligible Americans have bothered to contribute.

As you get older, you naturally pay more attention to retirement, so it's no surprise that people aged 45 to 54 have thus far been twice as likely to open IRAs as those between 25 and 34. But it's a major virtue of an IRA that the further you are from retirement, the more the IRA's tax-deferred compound interest can work for you. You've seen the well-advertised figures. If a person aged 30 religiously contributes $2,000 a year for the next 30 years, and the money earns 10 percent in the IRA, he or she would have $360,000 before taxes at retirement (at 60). And if that person's IRA grew at 10 percent compounded over a 40-year period, he or she would then have almost $1 million. Perhaps true enough. But this book is meant to get you off the money-go-round. Though you must develop assets for your future financial security, there is a larger question at hand. It's not whether an IRA is good or not but whether you should presently contribute to an IRA. Answer: Absolutely. Probably.

It appears that people are foolhardy if they don't immediately contribute to an IRA. At least that's what the government, institutions with
a vested interest, and most of the media would have you believe. So
why aren't more people currently placing money in an IRA? And are
they making so serious a mistake?

History lesson #1: Remember priorities. The first question is not
whether you *want* to save, but whether you are *able* to save for retirement right now. If you're putting your two children through school,
are paying a hefty mortgage on your home, have been hit with major
medical bills, and just lost your job, retirement saving probably is, and
should be, the furthest thing from your mind. It might make no sense at
all to tie up what little savings you have in a retirement fund that
imposes substantial penalties for withdrawal.

And you shouldn't be made to feel bad if you can't place money in an
IRA, especially if you aren't sure what it is, what it will do for you, what
to invest in, or where to get one. The ads make it sound like an IRA will
make you wealthy in your old age. But those numbers are misleading.
While an IRA will certainly help you in later years, an IRA will only provide partial retirement benefits no matter how long you place money in
one because you will require so much more.

Example: Assume a couple would like to retire. They have $50,000
and realize that it would be impossible, because of inflation, for them
to retire comfortably on this amount of money. So they try "cryo-
genic investing," hoping a *very* long-term IRA will do the trick. They
invest their money, have themselves frozen in a special vault, and leave
instructions that they be thawed out in 100 years.

When the couple emerges from the vault 100 years later, they can
scarcely wait to telephone their broker and check the performance of
their IRA investments. With the help of a computer, the broker tells
them that their original shares of AT&T are worth $5,684,360; their
GM stock is worth $8,271,320; their 100 shares of Xerox are worth
$34,869,320; and their mutual fund investment has grown to over
$100,000,000. With each valuation they become more and more ec-
static, shouting, "We're rich! We're rich!"

Suddenly, the telephone operator cuts into the conversation with these sobering words: "Your three minutes are up; please deposit $10,000,000."

Does this mean those of you who have been placing money in an IRA are making a mistake? Or does this mean you shouldn't place money in an IRA? The answers are no and no.

If you determine that this is a time when you can save for retirement, an IRA is very likely one of the many financially smart ways to do it. Don't worry if you don't understand the nuances of the IRA, and don't worry about the kind of IRA investment. It isn't likely you are ever going to notice the difference, 20 years from now, between an IRA investment for growth and an IRA for income.

Don't be confused by all the publicity. Whether you used a bank or a mutual fund, whether you invested in the stock market or various kinds of limited partnerships, what is important is balancing your needs today with those of the future and doing something when you are able to.

What IRA you'll invest in will depend on what you are comfortable with, and that decision will come about intuitively. Again, there is no perfect (IRA) investment. If predictability is important, then you'll naturally lean toward the safety of an income-producing investment. For those of you who lack additional investment money, an IRA may be your only investment portfolio, and, it should be diversified. And if you're like so many people, you'll simply invest in whatever looks good at the time. If interest rates are falling and the stock market is rising, you'll invest in a growth mutual fund.

All these possibilities are appropriate, but it's important to remember that an IRA is but a tool. If you miss your IRA ride this year, there are always other years and always additional modes of transportation--as long as you do something sometime, and as often as possible.

As I stated earlier, this is not a book to show you how to build a watch but to help you tell time. In covering other types of tax-advantaged retirement plans, my primary purpose is to make you aware of the many alternatives and to comment on them, not to confuse you. Some of these choices will not be appropriate or available for you, but a brief discussion of each will demonstrate that if you really want to, you should be able to retire or become financially secure. There are now so many tools outside Social Security and your own private investing that it's hard to see how you can fail. You see, financial security is like a 5-pound steak; the only way you can eat it is one bite at a time, but first you have to open your mouth.

A Keogh (HR10) Plan

If you are self-employed or are in a partnership, you can set up a Keogh plan, which is a tax-deferred pension plan. You may contribute to both a Keogh and an IRA. Though similar, because both allow you to deduct your contribution and in both the investments grow tax deferred, you can contribute more to a Keogh than you can to an IRA. The current limit is the lesser of $30,000 or 25 percent of self-employment income.

If you're thinking about setting up a Keogh for your unincorporated business, you must also cover those employees who meet certain minimum qualifications. Be aware, however, that the total amount you spend on the contributions may more than offset the personal tax savings the Keogh offers you. But then again, if you do contribute to the Keogh, you can also place a personal voluntary contribution (not tax-deductible, but tax-deferred) in the Keogh. But maybe you wish to establish a defined-benefit Keogh instead, which entitles you to place even more into a Keogh. Do you want me to go on?

Off the money-go-round: Hire someone else to worry about the details. Bring in a good benefit consultant, or accountant, or financial planner to explain how the pros and cons apply to you. Don't try to become an expert. And if later on you are not happy with your present decision, you'll be amazed how easy it is to freeze your Keogh and shift your emphasis to other retirement methods.

A Deferred Plan 401(k)

The 401(k) is one of many qualified plans that can be set up by an employer for the benefit of employees. It allows employees to build up savings, which are paid out at retirement or on termination of employment. The employees pay taxes on this money only when they draw it out, usually at retirement; until such time, the funds accumulate tax deferred. The main feature of the 401(k) plan is that employees can shift a great deal of their income (tax) to a later date. Funds set aside in a 401(k) plan are considered "deferred compensation" and are not reported to the IRS as income. As with the IRA and Keogh plan, the income on the amount set aside is not taxable until the tax year the taxpayer withdraws money. And as with the Keogh, you can have a 401(k) and an IRA at the same time.

This is considered a profit-sharing plan, an agreement between a corporation and its employees that allows the employees to share in company profits. And because of this, there are complex discrimination requirements. Whether you are highly paid or not-so-highly paid, if you or your employer offers (or can offer) one of these plans you'll almost certainly want to channel into it all the retirement savings you can. Currently, not only can you place more money in a 401(k) than in an IRA, but also your company can match a portion of your contributions. In addition to your being able to borrow against this plan, many of the rules involving the withdrawal of funds from a 401(k) are more favorable than those for an IRA or Keogh.

Currently, 401(k) plans are the hottest ticket in town. In a recent article in my monthly *California Business* column, I noted that participants were actually excited about 401(k) plans, and this comment produced a lot of mail echoing the statement. One letter said, "Our international office has implemented the program at the beginning of this year. True to your article, all are excited and speak highly about the plan." Whether you have heard of them or not is not important: what is important is that they represent the fact that new forms of retirement planning methods are continually evolving. You cannot, and should not try to, keep up with all of them. Even when you think you're up on the latest, out comes something like subsection 408(j), permitting an employer to contribute to an IRA covering an employee. Or 408(k)(2), under which corporations must make contributions for each employee who has reached the age of 25 and has performed service for the employer during the calendar year and in at least three of the five preceding years.

If you are in a position of influence in your company, as soon as you have read or heard about an unfamiliar retirement plan, call the pros immediately. (Don't expect them to call you.) As long as you tell your advisors of your company's philosophy toward providing retirement benefits, and your employees' desires, you'll be able to determine quickly whether the latest types of plans are appropriate, and if they are, to implement them effectively.

Company-Sponsored Thrift Plans

Your employers may offer a thrift plan, sometimes called a savings plan or savings-incentive plan. A thrift plan invites you to make contributions, if you wish, of a portion of your salary — usually 2 percent to 6 percent, but sometimes more. The employer is committed to match your contributions, and many plans also allow you to contribute unmatched dollars, once you exceed the employer's maximum matching level.

Most thrift plans are set up as qualified plans and therefore also receive special tax treatment. Until you receive distributions from this or any qualified plan, you do not have to pay taxes on your employer's contributions or on the investment earnings. Since many thrift plans also allow you to make voluntary contributions with your after-tax dollars, at the time of distribution you get your own contributions back free of tax. You pay the IRS, at the ordinary income tax rate, on only the accumulated tax-deferred interest.

Got all that? Don't be confused ... if your company offers one of these plans and a 401(k), first choose the 401(k), then an IRA, then the thrift plan, then the voluntary contribution. Again, in my book there is no such thing as a mistake. All these plans will work hard for you, and toward your future security, as long as you do something when you are able.

A Tax-Sheltered Annuity 403(b) Plan

Employees of public schools and certain tax-exempt organizations have the option, with their employers' permission, to contribute to a tax-sheltered annuity, or 403(b) plan. Under a 403(b) plan, you enter an agreement with your employer to put a portion of your income into a retirement account. The account belongs to you and goes with you if you leave your employer.

You may be able to contribute much more to a 403(b) plan than to an IRA, but the rules are complex, and you have a narrower range of investment possibilities. If faced with an either/or proposition, there is no strong reason to prefer a 403(b) plan to an IRA. Since you can have both an IRA and a 403(b) plan, you might as well put your funds into an IRA up to the maximum and then turn to a 403(b) plan if you wish to or can shelter additional amounts for retirement.

Other Retirement Plans

There are, of course, other major qualified corporate retirement plans in which the corporation makes the contribution, not you. Some major plans also allow voluntary contributions. If a voluntary contribution is possible, it is often wise to use that option as well, for the money grows on a tax-deferred basis and the plan can act as "forced" savings. Additionally, all employee contributions are "portable"; if you leave the company early, you can take your voluntary contribution with you.

The major qualified plans include other types of profit-sharing plans and various pension and stock purchase plans. There are entire books devoted to analyzing and discussing these plans. Since decision making about these plans usually isn't required on your part, I'll leave the descriptions to those other books. But even if you read those texts, you'll still be tiptoeing in a minefield if you establish a plan without expert advice from a pension consultant.

Your individual investments will, of course, also contribute toward your retirement or financial security funds. However, because of the great number of investments available, I'll wait until chapters 8 through 11 to cover the world of individual investments.

THE DOING

Only you can "personalize" what the word *retirement* means to you. But I have learned through clients' experience that full retirement is usually traumatic at first. Of course there's the adjustment in life activities, but there is also the mental adjustment to living off your assets or money drawn from retirement plans. At first you feel vulnerable, perhaps even paranoid. And most of you tend to be very, very conservative.

As I've already said, there is nothing to worry about. You'll not only adjust, but also find hidden assets. You will find, if you haven't already, that you should never underestimate your own intelligence, creativity, and luck. For even if times become difficult, you will successfully work them through.

Many years ago I told a 72-year-old pediatrician he could never retire under his present financial circumstances. He was used to a high income but also to the high life-style that went with it; thus he had saved little. He was "tired," and in spite of the numbers, retired anyway. His major asset was his house, a personal asset in my book. He and his wife decided to sell it and move into something smaller and newer. They found a new condominium project and picked out a unit (a choice unit on the water) before the project was built. As it happened, the California real estate market had just started mushrooming. They were able to sell their home, purchase their new condominium, and still have a good deal of money left over. Without trained foresight, the condominium purchase was a stroke of genius . . . and luck.

Because they were now motivated to do something, I really believe they intuitively knew what to do. On a relative basis that purchase also increased far faster than their home would have, if they had kept it. Today, they enjoy a comfortable retirement.

James Bond and I have both learned never to say never again. But I also observed how much less pressure there would have been had this doctor started planning ten years earlier, even five years earlier! I know he and his wife came out okay, and you will too, probably because you read books like *The Money-Go-Round.* But I also know the statistics: that only 2 out of 100 people will be able to retire *comfortably.* I cannot change the world. However, I would be really pleased if each person who buys this book would be one of those two. I hope none of you will be forced to depend on a gift or inheritance, equity from your home, or just ingenuity or luck to be able to retire with dignity.

There may, however, be some good news in not being able to afford to retire; some of you may not want to anyway. A lot of people really like to work and can do so either part-time or full-time. Sometimes the need or desire to be productive well past retirement age can be a powerful advantage in financial planning for later years. The simple need to work can often force you to find new ways to pursue goals. A great example is a client who "retired" at age 40 with a net worth of $1 million. He had worked very hard for that money. Now 25 years later, he has a net worth of more than $30 million and has hardly "worked" at all. He remained active but put his *mind* to work instead.

• Chapter 4

RISK PLANNING

Just as you thought you finally got off the money-go-round, along comes an event that places you right back on. Another kind of event that is never "timely" — a lawsuit; a permanent disability; a major robbery; or the destruction of your house by fire, flood, or earthquake; whatever. If death can be said to have a silver lining — which I'd never say myself — it lies in the fact that though death may end our lives, at least it doesn't disrupt them. "Untimely events" do disrupt our lives, as well as the lives of others, no matter what we do to offset their impact. And unfortunately, the odds favor that one of these events will happen, at some point, to each and every one of us — as sure as the shortest person in a group will be the last to learn it's raining.

The choice we have to make is the *degree* of difficulty we will tolerate, how much disruption we will allow. To believe "It won't happen to me" is naive at best, and usually negligent.

One of the reasons I began this book with death and wills, depressing as those subjects may be, is that I believe in reality. And death, as I've said before, is the surest reality. But there are other events over which we have no control that will have a major impact on us, and that impact will often be financial. How can that impact be softened, made less severe? How can we hedge our bets against these emergencies, tragedies, crises, risky situations, catastrophes? It doesn't matter what you call them. What matters is how real you believe the possibility is of such untimely events occurring in your life.

I hope the discussion in the following pages will go a long way toward helping you develop a greater sense of reality. Once you've gained that sense, you won't be taken in by financial mumbo-jumbo because you'll know what steps you need to implement in order to prepare for untimely events. You'll see — just knowing you have begun to close, or have closed more securely, the doors against possible problems will give you greater freedom to invest for the future.

Look back at your financial plan. An accident, sickness, or casualty could render it useless by forcing you to liquidate assets or redirect your cash flow. I often made the point by saying, "What good is it to plan for the future when you forgot to insure your home, and it burns down?" Today I can give a very real example: one of our clients, a world-class architect, really did forget to insure his million-dollar home. You can bet that he mended his ways and is now prepared for the unpredictable.

Since we can't hedge against every conceivable event, the next best thing is to determine whether we are covered for the most obvious events and the ones which could be most financially devastating. (Here I go again . . . sticking to the basics that a lot of people overlook.) Risks that should be covered, and can be covered at a reasonable cost, are: loss of earning power, health expenses, casualty losses (i.e., auto or home damage), and liability for injury or damage to others.

LIFE INSURANCE

We might as well start this section by talking about the precautions we can take against the economic problems caused by death. As I noted earlier, death is a financial event only for others. The only way to avoid this problem is through insurance, either by taking out insurance on yourself or on someone else.

No matter which sort of insurance you choose, the object is the same: to ensure that your family can maintain the same standard of living despite the death of the wage earner or wage earners. A family with young children will need sufficient resources to provide for the surviving spouse, as well as for the raising and educating of the children. If a wage earner dies while there is a gap between what a family has and what it needs, that gap, without insurance, will remain unfilled. On the other hand, do not overinsure yourself, thus making death an occasion for profit. That brings up one of my own created expressions: "'Tis better to be more loved in life than in death."

Life insurance is your second "estate," intended to replace the one that you — because of your untimely and (of course) unfortunate death — did not have time to build. Life insurance is either the purchase of time or liquidity (quick cash without significant loss). If you are single and have no dependents, there is no reason to purchase time or liquidity . . . you don't need life insurance. And the same is true for a newly married couple, each with a career, as long as they are childless. If these people happen to receive group term insurance through their places of work, of course, there is no reason to spurn it, since they got it at no cost.

Now for the really big question, which everyone asks. "Just how much insurance do I need?" Don't feel guilty if you're "everyone." Recently, the chief financial officer of a major company came to my office, and he was just as perplexed by that question as the next guy. We all know that if we ask that question of an insurance agent we may well get a confusing answer designed not to inform but to sell a product. In short, a fiendish plot to keep us on that money-go-round.

But getting off the insurance money-go-round is simple. To determine how much life insurance you need, all you do is determine what after-tax income will disappear because of death. That gap, between last year's income, when the wage earner was alive, and this year's, now that he or she is gone, needs to be made up by insurance. If you believe your need for insurance really is "stop-gap" — that is, you don't plan for your family always to be dependent on life insurance proceeds (and you certainly shouldn't plan on it) — your best bet is temporary and/or renewable term insurance. As your assets grow and the insurance premium rises, you systematically decrease the amount of coverage.

If filling the "capital need" caused by untimely death is the first reason for buying life insurance, paying estate taxes is the second reason. An insurance policy creates investment money — liquidity — that can offset estate taxes and, in some states, inheritance taxes that come due at a person's death. Life insurance that serves this purpose means that your heirs won't have to liquidate a large segment of your assets in order to pay the government.

But estate tax planning need be no more difficult for most of you than any other part of the financial planning process. Changes in tax law have made the bite less severe; by 1987, for example, you'll be able to leave $600,000 to your heirs without having to pay any estate tax. The higher the value of your life insurance policy, however, the larger the government "take" will be. Thus, the decision you face is how large an estate you wish to leave your heirs and how much money you are willing to pay (perhaps indefinitely) for insurance premiums that, if unpaid, would increase your beneficiaries' inheritance. A policy worth $600,000 for the death of one parent, and $1,200,000 for the death of both, is usually sufficient to assure your children's financial security. If your estate exceeds these levels, your children can receive at least these amounts tax-free should you die, and I see no *economic* reason for most of us to maintain life insurance under these circumstances.

If a large illiquid asset, such as the family farm, had to be sold to pay taxes, however, there would be an economic reason to maintain insurance coverage. Permanent life insurance could be more appropriate. And if your family or holdings are so large that more sophisticated estate planning is required, again I recommend that you seek an attorney who specializes in estate planning.

You would also do well to consult with a financial planner or an insurance agent with a financial planning background to make sure your estate plan dovetails with the rest of your financial plan. (How to seek competent advisors is discussed in chapter 14.)

These advisors as well as your attorney can and should also discuss irrevocable life insurance trusts, "gifting" methods, recapitalization techniques, and more. All these things will help you reduce your estate tax bill. But always keep in mind your priorities: don't make lowering the amount of your IRS check your only or ultimate goal.

If the best estate solution is too expensive for you today, then go with an abbreviated version of this solution or find the next best. If you find the solution confusing, you should probably wait a while before deciding. Remember too, when an agent talks to you about life insurance as the only solution, he or she is *selling* a financial product and may well not tell you everything. How many times have you heard bankers telling customers that their savings rates are not very competitive, or insurance companies announcing that certain of their policies are great money-makers for the company but not any good for you? Many insurance companies would prefer to see you confused, that is, trapped on the money-go-round, unable to choose independently among the new, newer, newest policies those institutions offer.

In the beginning, there was whole life. Then came term, followed by variable and universal. During the past decade, new forms of life insurance have evolved: direct recognition life, vanishing premium life, second generation universal life, and current assumption whole life. The latest creation is flexible-premium variable life. While each of these products may serve some purpose for a few of you, don't be taken in by insurance jargon. If you do believe everything you read and hear about insurance, you might as well wait for the "perfect" policy, which will undoubtedly be named something like direct universal variable vanishing build-up all-purpose happy-happy family life.

Accidental Death Policies

As long as I'm having so much fun talking about death, I might as well continue on my "roll" (yes, this is a roll).

Accidental death insurance seems like a bargain. And it is, at least to insurance companies, because it seldom pays: death by this manner is highly infrequent, a reassuring thought when you're flying at 40,000 feet. These policies are often supplied as part of employer-provided group insurance or in connection with various travel association cards and credit cards, like American Express. Accidental death policies pay only if the accident meets certain criteria, such as the death being specifically related to travel and/or policies being purchased through a particular credit card.

In general, I do not recommend this type of insurance. The amount of life insurance you carry should depend on your dependents' *needs* (such as helping pay for estate tax purposes, as discussed above) and not on the cause of death. The premiums for this type of insurance are small, however — they are often included in credit card fees — so if this minimal, unnecessary expense makes you feel better, go ahead.

Group Term Life Insurance

I can't quit now ... so don't you!

Many of you probably have employer-paid group term insurance. You may have not realized it, but the premium cost of any insurance coverage above $50,000 is included in your W-2 (taxable) income. Although the government will likely lower the figure at some point, the first $50,000 of coverage has for many years been a tax-free employee benefit.

As illogical as it may seem, you might actually save money by obtaining your own coverage and declining the company's coverage above $50,000 — if it will let you. But in order to do so, you have to be the kind of person who (1) enjoys bargains, (2) does not want to be dependent on your employer's benefit program, and (3) loves taking physical exams and filling out insurance forms.

In the final analysis, the few dollars you save probably aren't important. Only 3 percent of you — that is, only 3 percent of policyholders' heirs — will collect on group term anyway. Remember, it self-destructs when you retire or around ages 65 or 70, and that's usually before you do. Chalk up another one for the insurance companies!

LIVING INSURANCE

Okay, that's it — I can finally stop talking about death and cover *living* events for which people may need insurance. You remember, those unexpected things we cheerfully face throughout our lives: catastrophes, emergencies, tragedies, etc. Insurance companies would have you believe that calamity lurks everywhere. I believe, however, that it's more important to focus on the areas of your life that carry the greatest risks, for in all likelihood you've been so busy being on the money-go-round that you haven't even covered the basics. And if you haven't dealt with basic risks . . . well, don't be surprised if you're knocked for a loop.

But bear in mind that my comments, reviews, and recommendations should be considered *supplements*, and not *substitutes* for those of your own insurance agents. My discussion is intended to help you become familiar with the important terms of your insurance policies and focus on the areas where changes may be necessary.

Risks, as I've said before, are part of living. Ideally you would be able to shift all your risks to insurers; however, in many cases that is either not feasible or prohibitively expensive. Managing risks, in short, encompasses not only adequate protection, but also reasonable cost. If your risk management is prudent, you'll attain a certain "comfort level" and be able to minimize actual losses. If you're not comfortable unless you have the maximum amount of insurance coverage possible, if that high level lets you rest easy, then have a good night's sleep.

Disability Income

Your most valuable asset is you ... and your ability to earn an income (which I'll be further discussing in chapter 7). While most of you have some form of life insurance, most of you have also overlooked insuring your earning power. Consequently, disability insurance should be at the top of your insurance list — especially since your chance of suffering serious disability is greater than the chance of premature death. Just find your age in the chart below, and play the odds.

Chances of Disability vs. Death

	22		$7^1/_2$	
	32	the chances	$6^1/_2$	times greater
If you	37	of disability	$5^1/_2$	than the chances
are age ...	42	of 90 days or	4	that you will die
	47	longer are ...	$3^1/_2$	this year
	52		$2^1/_2$	
	62		2	

Chances You Will Become Disabled Before Age 65

Current Age	Disabled at least 6 months	Disabled at least 1 year	Disabled at least 2 years	Disabled at least 5 years
22	34%	27%	22%	15%
30	33%	26%	22%	15%
35	33%	26%	21%	15%
40	32%	25%	21%	15%
45	30%	24%	20%	14%
50	28%	23%	19%	14%

Adequate disability protection is vital because it ensures you'll still receive income should you become disabled. A good rule of thumb is to purchase insurance that will provide 75 percent of your current after-tax income.

But be careful: disability policies are tricky. There are five factors you must consider while evaluating the quality of a policy: the elimination period (the time between the onset of disability and the payment of benefits); the length of the benefit period; the amount of the monthly benefit; the definition of disability; and the renewal of the policy's provisions.

If you are the do-it-yourself sort, five minutes in the library will yield five year's worth of reading on the subject. Or you can consult a financial planner or insurance agent. Keep in mind your goal: that you're *sure* to be covered if you become seriously disabled and can no longer work.

Some of you may find that you're already covered — often more than once — by worker's compensation, a group plan, an individual supplemental plan, or even an auto or liability policy. Others, however, may find disability insurance hard to come by or terribly expensive — government workers and entertainers, for example. And if you are financially secure, you probably won't be able to get it at all. Believe it or not, there *is* a common element among the members of these groups: the insurers' belief that once these people are on disability, usually at a fairly high income level, they have little incentive to return to work. Disability insurance, after all, is only intended to be a stopgap measure.

Health Insurance

You've heard the expression, "What is money when you haven't got your health?" I've got another expression of my own, "Where is your money when you haven't got your health (insurance)?"

Health insurance is not something you can forget about just because you're covered by an employee health plan. Those programs may not cover all your family, or they may be incomplete in other ways or incompatible with your family's individual needs. You'll want to shop for health insurance in the same way you would shop for life and disability insurance: with caution. Remember, the most important thing to anticipate and insure for is unforeseen *major* health problems, not the routine expenses of physical check-ups and dental examinations.

If you're already covered by a health plan, the first step you should take is to analyze its weak points. Is everyone insured who needs to be insured? Are you aware of current health problems within your family that should be covered but aren't? Are there problems you can anticipate because they show up frequently in your family or that of your spouse? Don't try to insure against every conceivable problem, but do try to think of obvious potential problems. If you travel to exotic places, for instance, you should be sure you're covered for the common exotic diseases in those areas.

Major Medical

In order to evaluate properly the quality of a major medical plan, you need to examine a few "key areas": co-insurance provisions, deductibles, lifetime payouts or annual reimbursement limits, and the schedule of benefits and premiums.

Don't become obsessed with getting a small deductible or a very low stop-loss (which limits your liability to a certain amount each year). Bear in mind that these figures represent a relatively small expense for self-insurance, and that you will be out of pocket no more than this predictable amount. Again, remember to keep your priorities in order. You need insurance for the REALLY BIG hospital bill that can spell financial RUIN: you don't need a policy that covers hangnails (unless, of course, yours are so special they strain the resources of modern science). Since most types of medical expenses are covered up to the policy's limits, I strongly recommend — if you can afford to self-insure in part — that you take higher deductibles and a high stop-loss and insure for at least $500,000.

I also recommend you don't get sick (see, I've got all kinds of practical advice).

Aside from major medical, you'll hear about plans called basic medical, comprehensive, medical, hospital indemnity, and so on. Leave it to the insurance companies to create plans (and names of plans) that cover everything. Since I am convinced that these products are part of the conspiracy to put you and keep you on the money-go-round, I suggest your individual situation will give you a perfectly adequate sense of what plan is good, or best, for you. If you are planning to have children soon, for instance, it would be wise to make sure you get maternity benefits.

Much of this hospitalization information is difficult to decode, and thus something you are not likely to understand all by yourself. So once again, you should talk to an expert and be sure to communicate your worst fears. I might add, too, that a good way to uncover typical medical insurance problems is to visit a hospital and ask a benefits person what they see as the most common areas of deficiency. *Then* you can come to an informal final decision.

Dental

Since dental insurance coverage is generally difficult or expensive to purchase on an individual basis, the employee group benefit can be valuable. The plans pay up to certain dollar amounts for routine and preventive dentistry and a few other dental services like dentures, crowns, and orthodontia. If you are covered by such a plan, use it.

PROPERTY INSURANCE

Property insurance is such a large topic it's going to be difficult not to trot out all those details I promised myself I would try to avoid. But let's get started anyway because we both know your insurance agent probably doesn't call you.

Homeowners' policies cover two areas of loss: loss due to damage to the dwelling, other structures, and contents and losses due to liability. Some tenants' policies also cover these areas.

The best kind of policy to have is an "all-risk" policy, which means, for a change, almost exactly what it says — that all risks are covered, except those specifically excluded: earthquake, flood, nuclear war, etc. I prefer this type of insurance because the coverage is inclusive rather than exclusive. With an inclusive policy, you won't have to panic when an accident befalls you because most of the time you'll be covered.

I also recommend that you obtain a replacement cost endorsement. This provision means that the insurer will pay for the full cost of replacing your home, even if the cost is more than the limits of the basic policy.

It's also a good idea to insure the contents of your home for their replacement cost. Most policies pay only actual cash value — the difference between an item's original cost and its depreciation. Household items depreciate very quickly, and in the event of a major loss, the difference between the insurance payment and what you *actually* pay to replace your personal property may be very high. A personal property endorsement generally adds 10 to 15 percent to the basic homeowner's premium, and it's well worth the additional charge if you can afford it.

Be aware that almost all insurers apply special limits to certain types of property. Coins and currency, for example, are covered only up to a given worth depending on the policy (and this includes loss of cash). Other kinds of property subject to special limits are your diamonds, furs, goldware and silverware, Rolex, Hasselblad, precious gems or metals, and the like. These specific items can be covered by a special articles "floater" or endorsement, however, if the property is valued by an appraiser at a specific worth. If you go this route, update the appraisal at least every five years so you won't lose appreciation, or lose out to inflation, in case of loss.

But here's a surprise. Since inflation rates have come down, a number of these items have actually *decreased* in value since your last appraisal. You may have insured your favorite teddy bear for $500 and conscientiously paid premiums on that amount, but if Pooh can now be replaced for $300, that's what the insurance company will give you.

Insure only those items that you would really replace if lost and those you use most often. Also look for other, less expensive ways to protect your valuables. Why pay high premiums on things that could stay in a safe-deposit box? Insurance companies have special lower rates for safely stored items.

Another wise move is to make a photographic inventory of your home. Take pictures room by room, and then take individual photos of high-value items such as antiques, furs, and jewelry. Store this inventory in a safe place away from home — at your office or in a safe-deposit box.

If you can save a meaningful sum in premiums by raising your deductibles to $500 or $1,000, do so. As you've probably heard, the first dollars of protection are the most expensive; higher deductibles reduce premiums. Besides, the insurance company might well drop your account if you put in too many small claims, fearing — and correctly so, according to the statistics — that you may soon be due for a big claim.

Liability Coverage

The second section of the homeowners' policy provides comprehensive personal liability coverage. This coverage covers losses — property damage, bodily injury to others — that you are legally obliged to pay because they occurred under certain circumstances at your home (or even away from home). Ask for high limits — you never know know how high your liability may be. These limits will be increased substantially if they are integrated with the excess liability policy discussed below.

Another message from the "you probably didn't know" department: a homeowner's policy covers the named insured, resident spouse, and anyone under age 21 in the care of any person already named. I recommend that both you and your significant other, or others, be identified by name in order to avoid any ambiguity regarding the definition of "resident spouse."

If you don't own a condominium and never will, skip this paragraph. But if you do, read on, for condos can have very confusing insurance terms. Under many condominium deeds — documents more properly called Covenants, Conditions, and Restrictions — the individual owner owns only air space: the condo's inner walls, built- in appliances, carpeting, and cabinetry are jointly owned. In other CC&Rs, however, the individual owns everything beyond the bare walls: paint, wallpaper, appliances, etc. To complicate the picture further, the master policy covering the condo building may insure some jointly owned property, or all of it, and some individual property. I could go on and on — from loss assessment coverage to deductibles on the master policy — but my point is made: there are major differences between condo policies and homeowner or tenant policies. Ask your insurance agent about your policy's coverage and cross-check that information with your association board.

Automobile Insurance

Next to your home, the second most valuable property you own is probably your car, be it a Rabbit or a Rolls. Again, you want to protect against the really big loss. In most cases, seek the upper insurance limits and the highest deductible. It's generally a better idea for the car owner to pay for the inevitable minor repairs and let the insurance company pick up the major tabs.

Risk exposure is another issue to consider. In almost every family, in my opinion, a very high exposure occurs frequently — every time one of the kids drives the family car. The car's *owner* may have legal liability in the event of an accident, not just the driver. If someone in the other car is injured, he or she can be expected to sue the person with the most assets, and chances are it won't be Junior.

There are two ways to reduce this risk exposure, aside from making the car off limits to your teenagers (good luck with *that* one). The first is to raise your liability limits with an excess liability policy discussed in the next paragraph. The second is available only for legally adult children and involves giving the auto to the child, registering it in his or her name, and then acquiring a separate insurance policy for the child. This solution, obviously, requires that you part with a substantial asset, and it will increase your insurance costs because a family policy with multiple-car discounts is less expensive than separate policies.

Excess Liability Insurance

This policy is designed to supplement conventional auto liability and homeowners' insurance. It provides additional protection if you are sued over dog bites, slander, bad driving, or a raft of other mishaps and misdeeds.

Whether this extra coverage makes sense depends on how worried you are about being sued. Don't forget, either, that having a lot of liability coverage can be an invitation to a lawsuit. But I believe nonetheless that this type of policy is a "must" for every one of you. Your risk isn't measured by your assets but by the amount of the *potential* claims against you. With personal liability coverage, the insurance company pays the legal bills if you get sued, and the award as well if the plaintiff wins.

Coverage levels start at $1,000,000 but require specific limits in your underlying auto and homeowner policies. If you are liable for damage, the auto or homeowner's policy will usually pay first; after that, the umbrella policy will pay up to its limit. Coverage is available up to $10,000,000. The cost of $1 million of excess liability coverage is often about $80 to $120, and that makes it probably the best buy in the insurance business. If you think there is the slightest chance of being involved in a lawsuit (auto liability is probably the biggest worry), don't pass up this kind of insurance. If you *are* sued, and you *aren't* covered, the plaintiff won't be the only one injured.

ECONOMIC INSURANCE

Personal insurance is intended to help you out when you suffer from a well-defined problem — an accident, say, or a robbery. But what can you do about recession? About inflation? A declining dollar? We'll get to more specific advice in these areas soon enough: in this section we're more concerned with theoretical strategies for dealing with economic crises, what I call "economic insurance." Although in most of your investments you'll be looking for potential profits — the accumulation of investment capital — when it comes to risk planning, you're still looking to preserve your capital.

If buying insurance is one of the best ways to prepare for *personal* hard times, diversifying your portfolio is one of the best ways to prepare for *national* or *global* hard times: inflation, recession, depression. The reason for diversification is obvious: you don't want to put all your eggs in one basket. If you divide your investment assets, say, among seven different investments, you're not going to take a beating in all of them. Seven such investment groups are: U.S. Treasury bills, bonds, or notes; a mutual fund invested in high-grade common stocks; real estate; high-grade, short-term or intermediate-term corporate or municipal bonds; a tax-deferred annuity; natural resources; and precious metals. Each of these investments hedges against a particular problem, and most of them are high in liquidity — meaning you can get your money out fast, and so can respond quickly to changes in the economy.

I'll deal with these and other investments in detail in chapters 8 through 10.

• PART III •

Accumulating For the Present ... and the Future

Chapter 5

The Great American Nightmare: Purchasing a Home

TO BUY OR NOT TO BUY

At one time almost everyone believed that he or she would own a home someday. But housing has gotten so expensive in the past two decades that the homeowning desire may not be as strong as it once was. For many people, however, a home still represents the most important part of that dream: a concrete, wood, stucco, or brick symbol of earning power. A house can be a measure of success, a permanent, secure center in an everchanging world. And it's all yours, if you don't count the banks, savings and loan, or seller financing or that generous loan from your parents or in-laws.

Equally important, to most people, is the fact that houses can be good "investments." But in most cases that should not be, in my view, a significant reason for purchasing a home; remember I called a home a personal asset rather than investment asset back in chapter 1. Unless you *plan* to sell your home (and perhaps use the one-time credit against profit, see chapter 13), it's just a personal asset that happens to have risen in value. Though appreciation may not be as reliable today as it was in the 1960s and 1970s, a wise home purchase can still be an excellent "noninvestment investment." You won't find many investments that are both utilitarian and financially sound, and the combination of these elements continues to make home buying a very attractive proposition.

Owning a home is not all sweetness and light, however; it is expensive. First of all, there's the hefty downpayment; then there are the mortgage payments, perhaps at a high interest rate, and maintenance, furnishings, property taxes, insurance ... the list goes on and on. It's true, of course, that the interest part of your mortgage payments are tax deductible, but that doesn't lower your expenses; some part of your dollar may be deductible, but the other part is *not*. And the deductible portion, of course, must be paid up front. You'll still have to come up with all the money every month.

One of the greatest fantasies I know is the belief that buying a house is a good tax shelter. And I have noticed for some reason doctors seem to be the greatest converts to this "theory." One of my doctor clients who had listened to a colleague's financial advice had gotten in the soup so deep that when I met him he was considering a fifth mortgage just to "keep afloat." He had forgotten about the associated costs of owning a home, like decorating, gardening, furnishing, and so on. Yes, he had plenty of "tax shelter," but at what price! A house is *not* a tax shelter. It does not give you that big a deduction or any depreciation, tax deferral, or tax credit. The first thing to think about when considering a house, consequently, is *why* you want a house and *whether* you can afford it ... all of it.

One of the most common questions I get is, "Should I buy or should I rent?" The living costs of rental are far lower than for purchase: you can rent a home for about half of what you'd have to pay in mortgage costs alone. You also would have more ready cash for investment purposes — the money you did not have to spend on the nondeductible portion of your mortgage payment, the downpayment, the closing costs, and the taxes and maintenance. When invested, these savings can earn money.

If you are currently a tenant, weigh the advantages of your situation against the advantages of owning a home or condominium. And if you're thinking of "trading up" to a more expensive home, be wary; there's no guarantee you'll be able to sell your house at a profit or that you'll be able to sell it at all. (In the middle 1960s, it used to be a rule of thumb that to break even, after selling expenses, you had to hold onto your home for five years.) If you buy before you're financially ready, you could end up cash-poor and unable to pay for those things you once took for granted. The answer to the question to buy or not to buy will depend on the stability of your job, your life-style, your ready cash, and your willingness to be tied up with a long and heavy debt.

Once again, the idea I'm stressing is that you must determine what you *value* — in this case, whether you need to own your living space. Don't let the marketplace, or family or friends, or the media decide for you. If you're a salesperson frequently on the road, you may feel it's not worth investing in a house. If you expect to be transferred by your company every two or three years, it may not make sense to buy and furnish a house — unless your employer will help you sell the house, move, and buy a new house. If renting month to month, or even leasing by the year, makes you fearful of eviction or of becoming a wandering minstrel, you may want to start an investment program targeted toward a house downpayment. If you just feel good about the idea of owning your home but can't explain why, then it's still the right thing for you. If living in the "right" house is important to your career, that too can be a legitimate consideration.

TYPES OF HOUSING

If you determine that buying a house does make sense for you, think about what sort of house you'd like, in what area, at what price. Must you live in an overpriced part of town because some of your peers *like* to pay more than they need to? You don't have to do what "everyone else" is doing. It's not compulsory for single people (swinging or otherwise) to live in condominiums, or for young couples to buy "starter" houses, or for large families to live in suburban developments. A real estate agent may steer you toward certain kinds of housing because his or her other clients in the same age bracket have wanted similar things, but that doesn't mean *you* must follow the crowd.

Let's look at starter homes for a moment. You may have grown up in a single-family house in suburbia with multiple baths, multiple bedrooms, multiple dens, and multiple blades of grass. Today, you may simply not be able to afford such a house, even if you wanted it — which many people these days do not, rejecting the traditional single-family house in suburbia in favor of central, urban quarters nearer their places of work. Alternative housing is springing up everywhere: new forms of the "Great American Dream" are beginning to appear in cities and towns all over the country. Innovative and more affordable homes are being built, and housing approaches once thought passé are now being reconsidered.

Cluster Housing

"Cluster housing" is one of the most popular and fastest-growing alternatives to the single-family home on its own lot. Cluster housing can take many forms: condominium apartments, attached suburban row homes or townhouses, even a new generation of multifamily dwellings.

The advantage of clustering over single-family detached housing is mostly economic. Because clustering greatly increases the economy of scale, a builder can offer a far greater number of amenities than a traditional house can. Many condominium developments offer community pools, recreation centers, media rooms, secretarial services, and a lot of other things wrapped up in one affordable package. A Northwestern University survey of condominium owners found that 85 percent were extremely satisfied with the upkeep of their homes, their level of privacy, and their neighbors. A condo in such a development could be a good starter home.

Downsized Homes

Recognizing that many potential buyers do not want or need the spaciousness of the typical single-family home, many developers are building miniaturized homes. Builders report that small homes of one and two bedrooms and floorspace of 1,000 square feet are outselling the more traditional houses three to one — and no wonder, with prices as much as $20,000 less. You must, of course, be willing to park your cars outside — a garage would double the size of your home and make it much more costly.

Tandem Homes

A tandem home looks very like a traditional single-family home and is constructed in essentially the same way. The tandem, however, is designed to accommodate *two* families. Each owner has a master bedroom, bathroom, and sitting area, but they share the home's entrance, living/dining area, and kitchen.

This housing solution is especially suited to older people or young working people. And it can also be excellent for separated couples who are still somewhat compatible; they can see each other only when they want or need to.

Expandable Homes

In many ways, an expandable house is just an unfinished product. In exchange for building a home for as little as $40,000, developers will omit extras like dishwashers and carpeting and leave the house with the basement and spare rooms unfinished. In theory, the homeowner can complete the rooms and add amenities (walls, floor, roof?) whenever he or she can afford to.

Build-it-Yourself

Back in the late 1910s and early 1920s, as I recall, Sears used to sell build-it-yourself home kits for $1,500. The kits turned into fairly large homes and many are still standing and quite desirable.

Well, the theory today is that you are less skilled and so can't build your own home unless you first sign up for 48 hours of lessons at a cost of $300. Authorities estimate that the novice homebuilder can erect (with help from subcontractors) a 1,500-square-foot structure at a cost 20 to 60 percent below that of a comparable prebuilt home.

Floating Homes

One of the most exotic forms of alternative housing, and certainly the most aquatic, is the "floating home." Unlike the more familiar houseboat, a floating home cannot move under its own power: it must be towed by a boat or tug. Built on barges, these homes come in all different sizes, from postage stamp to split-level mansion. They are slightly less expensive than their land-based counterparts, and in some areas — it seems only natural — you won't have to pay any property tax.

There are, of course, many other forms of shelter of which we're all aware: mobile homes, prebuilt factory homes, and more. Though clearly not in the tradition of the suburban, single-family, detached dwelling, they help fulfill the continuing Great American Dream of homeownership. If you want more information on these possibilities, visit your local library.

MORTGAGES

If you know exactly what house you want, the next step, of course, is to get financing. Easier said than done. Banks and savings and loans, it seems, have been taking lessons from the insurance industry: Banking 101 must be "How to confuse and create dependency," or "Keep 'em on the money-go-round."

Once upon a time, borrowing money was a fairly predictable thing. You would go to a bank, say you wanted a loan, prove you didn't need it, and before too long you'd get it. Now, however, things are completely different, except for the fact that you still have to show you don't really need the money. Houses are selling at many times their original prices, interest rates have increased dramatically, and the once-standard home mortgage now comes in almost as many varieties as there are colors of house paint. Sorting through them is a superhuman job, yet there are some basic elements of a mortgage that everyone should know. The better grasp you have of the mortgage concept, the better questions you'll ask, and the better application you'll make — for *your* goals, not the seller's.

The *downpayment*, of course, is the complement of the mortgage: the cash you pay up front. Generally, the lower the downpayment, the better since the more money you keep, the more money you have to invest. An awful lot of people today, however, are tired of paying (seemingly) forever and are opting to make larger monthly payments in order to pay off the home in a shorter period of time. A mortgage for 15 years or less is not uncommon. Early free-and-clear ownership is especially of major value if it also helps you sleep better at night.

Adjustable-Rate Mortgages

Adjustable-rate mortages, or ARMs, are probably the best-known of the new breed of "creative financing" mortgages, though there are several mutant ARMs, the latest of which are "convertible" home mortgages. I will cover the two most common. With the basic ARM, the interest rate you pay varies according to an accepted economic index, such as Treasury bill interest rates, money market rates, cost-of-fund rates, or the Home Loan Bank Board's average of mortgage rates. Experts say it is impossible to predict which index will prove most beneficial over the long term to either borrower or lender, but they agree that borrowers should avoid mortgages tied to the savings and loan industry's cost-of-fund index. That index is sure to rise over the long term as savings and loans periodically raise the rate of interest paid to depositors.

Depending on how the mortgage is set up, your monthly payments may change in many ways. They may move up and down in tandem with the index rate, or remain the same, with the length of the loan increasing or decreasing. Lenders have a lot of latitude in floating-rate mortgages, compared to the old fixed-rate mortgages, and that means potential homeowners must be alert to the constantly changing terms of the loan.

Even the "simple" adjustable-rate mortgage can be difficult to comprehend, compare, and predict, and that's why I dislike them. With fixed-rate mortgages you set the total price of the loan in advance, and that means you can plan for the future knowing exactly what your risk is. If you are an incurably optimistic borrower, however, or plan to sell your home within, say, four years, a change in rate should not seriously affect you, so an ARM might be for you.

With a *graduated-payment ARM*, the second most common adjustable-rate mortgage, your payments are lower in the early years and higher in the later years, the theory being that you will make more money as you grow older. If you are lucky (or unlucky) enough to get such a mortgage — perhaps you and your loan officer sing the same college fight song — you may discover that your payments aren't even covering interest costs. After two or three years of such a mortgage, the money you still owe may be greater than the principal you borrowed! Unless you're sure double-digit inflation is around the corner, that's not a very good way to build home equity.

Rollover and Balloon Mortgages

Some of the most controversial of mortgages are rollover and balloon mortgages. They are similar to the home loans popular in the 1920s, before the ascendancy of the fixed-rate mortgage. Many experts say these loans were a primary cause of foreclosures during the depression.

Monthly payments on a rollover mortgage are set almost exactly as they are for a traditional 25-year or 30-year fixed loan. Rollover mortgages, however, must actually be paid in a much shorter time, usually within three to five years. At the end of the term, the borrower must either pay off the loan in a lump sum or refinance.

In California these loans became so popular at one point that it was said that half the state would come due in five years. As luck would have it, many properties did appreciate and interest rates were lower when the balloons came due. Most borrowers therefore were able to favorably refinance their properties.

The necessity for refinancing is the reason for calling this mortgage a "rollover." If the loan officer chooses *not* to refinance the loan and insists on full payment at the end of the term, he has given you a "balloon" mortgage and you should immediately put a hex on him. It's best to stay away from this sort of mortgage if you can help it; financial planner Venita VanCaspel mentions in one of her books that mortgages with balloon payments have been referred to as "neutron loans" because they leave the building standing but kill the owner.

Rollovers are fine if you can ensure refinancing or manage to sell the house before the lump sum is due. If you can't do that and can't make the final payment, it's certain — you lose your equity and your house.

Shared-Equity Mortgages

Also called a "partnership mortgage," a shared-equity mortgage allows a buyer either to purchase a house with no downpayment or to purchase one that is 40 percent larger than he or she would otherwise qualify for with a conventional mortgage. The key to the plan is that it provides the investor "partner" with a two-for-one tax write-off. The buyer — the person who takes possession of the house — and the investor enter into an agreement under which the two become coequal in the obligations of the mortgage but in which the buyer remains the dominant partner. The tax benefits are shared equally by the partners, but the buyer receives all the other benefits of home ownership.

Another new form of loan is the shared-appreciation or shared-equity mortgage. Essentially, the lender gives the borrower a lower interest rate in return for sharing in the ownership of the house (shared equity) or in the expected increase in its value (shared appreciation). The lender takes its share of the profit when the house is sold or refinanced.

I believe this sort of mortgage will be the wave of the future. But like the ARMs, the advantage lies primarily with the loan institution.

Mortgage Buy-Downs

In this arrangement, the builder "buys down" the mortgage interest rate for two or three years by paying part of the loan himself. After that, the interest rate returns to a predetermined level or to the going market rate. Although the buy-down is strictly short term, many developers believe the device can make a home affordable to financially strapped potential buyers.

Assumable Mortgages

If you're not buying a newly constructed home, you may be able to get an *assumable mortgage* — where you take over the mortgage payments from the house's previous owner. If the seller has owned the house for some time, the interest rate is likely to be quite low, but the equity he or she has built up in the house will be correspondingly high. In order to assume such a mortgage, the lending institution cannot have a prohibition against the assumption of an existing loan, and your downpayment will have to match that built-up equity. If that sum is large, even if it is assumable, you may wish to consider a new mortgage, or arrange a loan directly with the former owner. For unless you are trying to pay off your mortgage quickly, it may not be the best use of such a large block of capital.

If you're overwhelmed by this vast array of mortgages — I haven't even made a dent — then financial institutions have indeed succeeded in keeping you on the money-go-round. But it need not be so tough. If you can find a fixed-rate mortgage, in all likelihood that should be your first choice. If the interest rate or downpayment is too steep, however, you should consider, in tandem with a financial advisor, the alternatives that remain open to you. Keep in mind that your primary goal is getting a mortgage that you and your significant other are comfortable with, and remember, too, there is no such thing as a mistake. Although "this home is forever," as we all say, chances are very high you'll not stay in your home more than five years anyway.

You now have "Larry's More-or-Less Complete Guide to Buying a Home." Dog-ear these pages, refer to them often, and show them to your friends and enemies alike. When you get the homebuying "itch," reread this chapter — and then take a cold shower.

Chapter 6

THE KEY TO ACCUMULATING ASSETS

It makes no difference whether you are just starting to invest or have been investing for many years. It's all the same. You want to feel confident about your investment decisions even if you don't think you know a lot about investing. However, it's usually a very intimidating experience. And to encourage that feeling, there are literally thousands of investments to choose from, and hundreds of *types* of investments, with as many as 20 new ones appearing on the scene each day.

Just when you've reached a decision to buy something that's guaranteed by the government, you discover there are practically an infinite variety of government-guaranteed investments on the market. Everything from zero coupon bonds to EE savings bonds; from Ginnie Maes to straight Treasury issues; from short-term, to intermediate, to long-term maturities; from tax-free investment income to tax-deferred income; from bonds fully backed by the full faith and credit of the U.S. government to issues backed only by the *expectation* that the government will act as guarantor. Should I go on? The extent of investment possibilities can be, and usually is, a great headache. Money-go-round wins, by a TKO.

The major reason for investing is the hope of receiving a greater return in the future. The *key* to investing, and actually *achieving* that desired result, is — that's right — a good plan. If your financial plan is a road map, investment is the vehicle that gets you to your destination. And to take the analogy a little further, you need the right *kind* of vehicle — one that reflects your style, keeps you comfortable, and is capable of giving everything you ask of it. You'd probably prefer to drive a four-wheel-drive station wagon over a snowy mountain pass than an open convertible. By the same token, when traveling coast-to-coast you're likely to prefer a comfortable, smooth-riding car to a pair of roller skates. If you keep your destination in mind, and how long it will take to reach that goal, you'll have a pretty good idea of what kind of vehicle you should buy and which kind would suit your personality. And you should not, of course, limit yourself to one vehicle; in the investment world, you can buy different modes of transportation for each goal in your life!

Unfortunately, however, many people don't have financial plans. These people end up investing their money in whatever seems "reasonable," basing their choices not on their own goals, but on the persuasiveness of the salesman or the popularity of the product. That's the reverse of what an investing strategy should be; it's taking the test before you've studied the lesson.

WORDS OF GENERAL WISDOM

In the next few chapters I'll discuss many of the instruments you might consider. But don't put on blinders. And don't get caught up in the details, either. What you'll be looking for is whether the ideas seem applicable to your situation. What I'll be giving is commentary that should help you decide for yourself. Many ideas will seem appropriate, but remember, one size does *not* fit all.

After you have determined your goals, you will have to bear in mind the amount of money you are willing to invest, your age, your personal preferences, the preferences of your spouse or significant other, and so on. Then think about your stage of life. At each stage there is a financial and an emotional juncture.

If you're young and single — say, 23 to 35 — your portfolio may be more oriented toward greater risks: you may not have the expense of raising children and probably aren't thinking much about retirement. At this stage of your life the key issues are love (lots of it) and work, and most of your plans are for the present. If you lose money, you're not worried very much because you know you can replace it fairly quickly. And besides, time is on your side.

If you're married, in your late 30s to 50s, and have a couple of kids, you may require additional income for college expenses. You may even have started to think about retirement. You'll have more assets to protect and your orientation has evolved: you're more concerned about the future. The portion of your portfolio geared toward growth or risk may have declined from the 85 percent of your young singlehood to 50 percent today.

If you're between 51 and 65, you may be spending a lot of money — traveling, helping out your grown children — and getting ready for retirement. You certainly want to keep what you have, and you're not sure you have enough. Growth investments may now take up only 35 percent of your portfolio, a ratio that may decrease even more when you retire. Income, not growth, becomes of primary importance because of the need to replace your paycheck. Once you've turned 65, you may want to start "passing the torch." You're entering years, perhaps, of divestiture, of learning how to let go.

I am aware that none of these examples may properly reflect your situation. I have clients in their 20s and 30s who have been banking every dollar they can toward their retirement years. I have clients in their 70s embarking upon a major construction project as a long-term investment. Look at George Burns — he has entertainment commitments past age 105. But you get the idea; though everyone has different goals, personal investment decisions are usually dictated to a large extent by the investor's age. If you're like most of us, the first really serious "pause for concern" occurred, or will occur, on your 40th birthday. Then there's the magic 50, 60, 65, 70, and so on (we all hope).

After you've thought about your current stage of life, the next step is to find out what's available in the marketplace. It's just like buying a road vehicle; ideally, you'll start looking at brand names only after you've determined what kind of transportation you want, whether it's a truck, a station wagon, a sedan, a sports car, roller skates, or a camel.

The specific, detailed information you need before you buy can be obtained from a good professional financial advisor (see chapter 14). Specialized current books, radio and TV shows, and advisory newsletters can also be a major help, as can a number of investment magazines. For example, in *Money, Sylvia Porter's Personal Finance, Fact, Forbes,* and *Changing Times* magazines, as well as the "Money" section in *USA Today,* I have found a lot of high-quality, useful, and specialized information. "Your Money Matters" column in the *Wall Street Journal,* and the quarterly financial Sunday supplements in the

New York Times, even your local newspaper's business section are marvelous places to look for this sort of information. Additionally, syndicated columnists Dan Dorfman and Robert Metz are but two of the numerous columnists who provide insightful information.

You'll note that while I mentioned financial information sources by name, I have refrained from mentioning any "brand name" investments. Why? Because I know it's more important for me to stress the principles of investing. You will be able to get all the brand names you want just by standing on the roof and yelling, "I'm ready!" Remember, you've been on the money-go-round because all this time "they" have been ready — not you. School's now in session and now you can be your own guru. You can, and will, ask yourself whether an investment fits into your overall plan, what its practical effects will be. And you won't expect more of an investment than it can deliver.

There are four basic benefits available in an investment: safety of principal, tax advantages, current income, and capital preservation. No investment contains all four — in fact, the more the investment contains of one element, the less it contains of another. You can't have an absolutely safe principal and a high growth potential at the same time: in short, trade-offs are unavoidable.

Many financial planners — including me — use a common analogy developed by Richard Wollack to illustrate the trade-offs of prospective investments.* An investment is like an orange: there's only so much juice in it. If each of the four benefits above is represented by a 4-ounce glass, and each investment produces 8 ounces of economic "juice," you won't be able to fill up all four glasses. You can put 2 ounces in each glass, or 4 ounces in two glasses, or some combination in between, but you'll never get more than 8 ounces of juice from that orange.

---

* Published in *Tax-Advantaged Investments* by Richard Wollack and Alan Parisse (Consolidated Capital Communications Group, 1982); and in "The Orange Juice Analogy," *The Digest of Financial Planning Ideas,* April 1985.

The "Orange Juice" Model

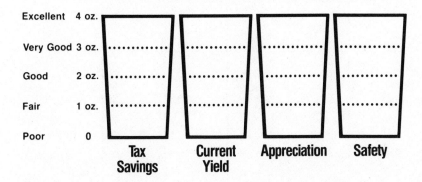

Let's say that each glass represents 4 points, and that the best score an investment can achieve in a benefit category is also 4 points. Our orange juice grading scale would look like this:

4 points = Excellent (among the top 20 percent of all investments in providing this benefit)

3 points = Very good (better than 60 percent to 80 percent of all other investments in providing this benefit)

2 points = Good (better than 40 percent to 60 percent of all other investments in providing this benefit)

1 point = Fair (better than 20 percent to 40 percent of all other investments in providing this benefit)

0 points = Poor (among the bottom 20 percent of all investments in providing this benefit)

This rating scale assumes, and properly so, that every investment provides a finite amount of the four basic benefits: tax sheltering, current yield, appreciation, and safety. (In many cases, of course, there will be *no* score in one or more benefit categories.) The scale is intended to help you focus on your objectives in choosing an investment, not on performance.

Investment Objectives Rating Model®

High Quality Municipal Bond

Look at the completed diagram for the high-quality municipal bond analyzed on this page. The diagram shows my rating of the bond as follows, with explanations:

Safety: A high-quality municipal bond is among the safest of investments (4 points).

Tax Savings: While municipal bonds produce tax-exempt income, their tax advantages are not as high as those produced by high write-off partnerships (2 points).

Current Income: Municipal bonds provide good — but not outstanding — benefits (2 points).

Appreciation: Municipal bonds do not appreciate, and their value may even decline in the face of rising interest rates (0 points).

Using the same rules and principles, you can rate real estate or any other investment.

Now it's your turn. Using your finest artistic talent, draw a blank diagram like the one we just looked at and distribute the economic benefits from a proposed investment. (If you don't know where to begin, read up on the particular investment you want to analyze or seek the help of a professional financial advisor.) You could also do the same with an existing investment. Do the diagrams match your financial profile? Are the benefits you're getting from your investment appropriate to your stage of life and individual situation? If you have high current income, for example, you may wish to fill the tax-savings glass; if you are planning to send your two young children to college, you might value long-term appreciation. By making individual diagrams for each of your investments, you'll know exactly where you stand with each of them; by making a master diagram based on these individual analyses, you'll know exactly where you stand with each of the investment benefits.

These diagrams should help you understand both the basic axioms of investing and the trade-offs involved in choosing the investments that best meet your needs. If you don't need current income, why pick an interest-producing investment over one that potentially produces growth?

JOHN BROWN REVISITED

The types of investments I'll be talking about in later chapters are generally arranged from the safest to the least safe — from interest-bearing instruments (government, bank, and bond investments) to income and/or growth vehicles (stocks and mutual funds); from precious metals and natural resources to tax shelters; from venture capital investments to commodity futures. This drive through the investment woods obviously is not a straight one, and that's because each investment type has unique strengths and weaknesses.

What you need is financial perspective, and that means deciding for yourself what you want from your money. I know it's fun to find out what other people are doing with their finances, but it's more important to know what *you're* doing with yours. And the sooner you do it, the better; once you've established your goals, you should implement your plan as soon as possible. If we look at our example of John Brown, we can see how much better off he could have been had he implemented a plan ten years earlier.

John, at 42, realized he had some major expenses ahead of him, expenses he hadn't really thought about until he created a life plan. If he's lucky, he'll be able to scrape up the money with which to pay for all of them; if he's not, he may have to delay his goals. But luck doesn't *have* to enter into such calculations; if John had begun to think about and plan for his goals ten years earlier, he might have peace of mind today. His immediate goals at the time, you may recall, were these:

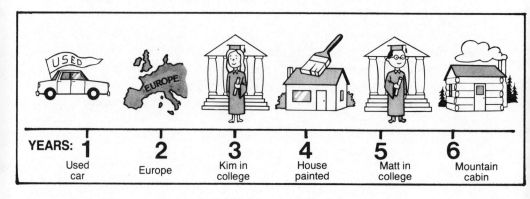

YEARS: 1	2	3	4	5	6
Used car	Europe	Kim in college	House painted	Matt in college	Mountain cabin

If we turn the clock back those ten years, John will at least have a sharper view of the future and much more time in which to accumulate assets to meet those goals.

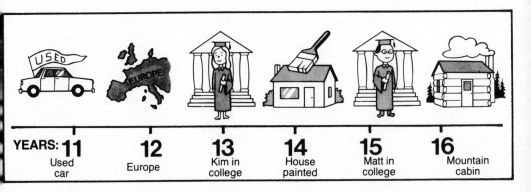

YEARS: **11** **12** **13** **14** **15** **16**
Used car | Europe | Kim in college | House painted | Matt in college | Mountain cabin

Naturally, he couldn't have been ready for everything — having another child earlier than he and his wife expected, for instance — but he could have budgeted enough so that his fixed expenses, and then some, were paid for. And meanwhile, he could have been investing in his dreams to earn the money for his unfixed expenses down the line.

In the following chapters I'll discuss many investment possibilities.

• Chapter 7

HOW INVESTING WORKS

Just as we're getting to the exciting part — investing your money — I'm afraid I have to put on my black hat and be the bearer of bad news. Successful investing is not exciting, nor should it be. It is a long, oh-so-slow, boring process. It's about as exciting as paying bills. No wonder so many of you want someone else to do it for you! Money excitement is why so many of you go to Las Vegas, Atlantic City, the racetrack, or poker parlors or put a few bucks in football pools or state lotteries. Because you can cut out the middlemen ... the long wait to see how well you did. You move directly from the starting gate to the finish line without having to endure all those steps in between.

Some of you love the thrill of competitive gambling and will always be ready to "bet the house, spouse, and kids." And if you lose ... well, you'll just start over. But I know most of you don't like such high risks. And why should you? Surprise — exciting as it may seem, "get rich quick" just doesn't work. Bernard Baruch said it best: "When hopes are soaring, I always repeat to myself, two and two make four and no one has ever invented a way of getting something for nothing." In all my years in dealing with people and their investments, I have yet to see anyone succeed quickly on purpose. Those who did succeed quickly never set out to: they were careful, methodical, and basically conservative people. They understood that successful investing is a one-step-at-a-time process. Nothing more, nothing less.

They never wager the house. They understand, instead, that when you're trying to burn a very large, very thick log, a single match is no match for it at all. As with investing, the first thing you need is a small flame — something to light some paper, which you then use to ignite small twigs, which in turn can fire up kindling, and then larger logs. Now you have a fire large enough and hot enough to burn a log of any size. A small ember can sometimes ignite a large log, but how many times have you seen that happen?

Both the match that starts the fire and the fuel that enables it to grow come from your income, from *you.* You must therefore bear in mind throughout the investment process that you are your number one investment. No investment will ever be able to perform as well as you, for only you can create an infinite increase in the value of your investment each year. On January 1 your "asset," you, has created no earnings, but by December 31 this asset has outperformed *every* investment ever made.

This unsurpassed earning power is why I say you should always invest in yourself first. Your money and/or time should first be spent upgrading your earning skills, not on the other investments. And try to do what you really enjoy. People who make a lot of money generally love what they are doing.

Your earning power is *enormously* important, for the more you earn, the more money (in theory) you should be able to place in new investments. New investments, and new money placed in old investments, will gradually provide the firepower needed to reach your goals. An increase in value from your early investments alone will simply not be great enough to meet your goals: the rate of increase will be far too low. If you don't save money over time and don't add that new capital to your investment assets, achieving your goals would require an uninterrupted aftertax annual return of something like 20 to 50 percent.

There are advisors who constantly talk about those kinds of returns. But talk, we know, is cheap and can cause its own problems. Our too-high expectations often influence our investment decisions, consciously or unconsciously, and that's rarely good. Anything short of the expected 20 or more percent may lead you to believe you are falling behind, and you probably are if those are your only investments.

You are your number one best investment, and the addition of new capital to your portfolio provides your *second* best investment performance. Your excess cash flow *instantly* creates, say, a $5,000 investment. But an existing $5,000 investment takes several years to reproduce itself. Get my point? This is why professional financial advisors often say, it's not what you make but what you keep. And don't blame income taxes, they aren't the only culprit. Most of the time it's your spending habits. Example: I have a client who earned $50,000 but spent $60,000 last year; he maintains he always lives within his income, even if he has to borrow to do so!

In George Clason's *The Richest Man in Babylon,* my client would find a soulmate. One character says that "what each of us calls our 'necessary expenses' will always grow equal to our income, unless we protest to the contrary." And in Dickens's *David Copperfield,* the impecunious Mr. Micawber says, "Annual income twenty pounds, annual expenditure nineteen six, result happiness. Annual income twenty pounds, annual expenditure twenty pounds ought and six, result misery."

Even if you do add new capital from time to time, however, the numbers may lead you to believe, at times, that you are still falling behind. Some of you may then feel you have to play "catch-up," and that's really a mistake. You may believe you're falling behind because you're looking at each investment in isolation — another mistake — instead of looking at the overall picture. You should measure your "performance by objective": how your portfolio as a whole is doing in relation to your goals. If you're measuring your "performance by the numbers," you're examining each tree while overlooking the forest.

Some investments may appear to be falling behind, or may even be causing a loss. Sell? Doubtful — look at the reason you bought the losing investment. If your objective in buying was to "hedge" or "insure" your portfolio, it is probably still doing its job. If you purchased gold for that purpose, for example, your intention was to offset possible losses in other investments due, perhaps, to rising inflation. Just because those other investments are performing well, and gold is dropping in value, does not mean you should sell it: do you sell the kitchen fire extinguisher after you've managed to cook one meal without burning down the house? The extinguisher, like the gold, was purchased for a purpose and remains reliable even though it hasn't been used. It should stay in place unless you alter your reasons for holding it (see chapter 12 for a further discussion of precious metals).

If you invested money in a growth mutual fund and found it grew at "only" 10.4 percent, well under the 21.66 percent average annual return of the previous five years, again that does not mean that you should sell. Unless you're aware of a problem unique to that particular fund, this investment should be viewed in context with your other investments. Ask yourself, "How are my investments performing overall, including the new capital I've put in, based on the goals I've set?"

Now you can see why it is so important to set well-defined goals. But they must be goals you can relate to. When your goal is this intangible thing called "financial security," it's very difficult to gauge your progress. The goal is too distant, too hazy; it moves around too much. It's like trying to grab a handful of air.

Let's take an example. If you presently live on $2,500 a month, 20 years from now it would cost you $7,295 a month to live the same way you do now, assuming an inflation rate of only 5¹/₂ percent. Think about it: can you see yourself currently spending more than $7,000 a month? If you are already spending that much, can you picture yourself shelling out more than $25,000 a month?

If you are of a certain age, you may remember a 1930s insurance advertisement — once famous, now infamous — that read, "How I retired on $100 a month." Can you imagine your reaction if a person had turned to you at the time and suggested that within the next 20 or 30 years you would need $1,000, or $1,500, or more than $2,000 a month to maintain your financial security? Impossible!

Many of you will recall your reaction some years ago when forecasters suggested that you would someday spend more than $10,000 for a Ford or Chevrolet. You paid "only" $3,000 for one 15 years ago, and a top-of-the-line Cadillac could be had for $6,500. Hard to relate to a five-digit car price, wasn't it? Today, most cars are in that range.

I have a copy of a 1969 *U.S. News and World Report* article taking a long look at what inflation might bring. Man's haircut — price now: $2; year 2000: $10. Food for four — price now: $40 per week; year 2000: $112. Having a baby — cost now: $200 for obstetrical care; year 2000: $640. It seems like the year 2000 occurred about 1982!

These figures certainly give us a measure of changing times but not a useful one. Long-term goals have a meaningful function, but you first need to establish accurate short-term goals you can measure and relate to. Though you know your long-term goal is financial security, you will only succeed if you first achieve your short-term, concrete, relatable goals. It's like sailing: your home may be halfway around the world, but until it's directly in view, you must decide on various ports of call on route. At each port you can take your bearings, adjust your course, and enjoy the fact that you've come so far.

When clients insist that I project their investment performance for the next 20 years, the computer is happy to oblige. If they really believe this analysis provides financial security, I put on my (well-worn) black hat and point out that the world does not stand still. The long-term projection is really no more reliable than the computer paper it's printed on. This collection of numbers and words is good only for creating false impressions and encouraging complacency. You can plug in any assumption you wish and play with the numbers until they provide security. If something goes wrong, sue the computer. But the real world is today — it's not bright numbers on a screen.

If your long-term goal is to set that very large log ablaze, but you can't envision your match doing the job, concentrate on the smaller blaze that will accomplish nearer-term goals. You will find that the blaze will grow even as you accomplish those goals, and that the fire will be plenty big enough to handle your longer-term goal, when it draws close.

So how, today, can you determine and relate to what will constitute financial security 20 years from now? Again, I ask you not to get caught up in the details. But I do recognize that "trust me, you'll make it if you concentrate on your immediate goals" is not always a good enough explanation. So, with my next "Trust Me" section, I will provide some back-up information as well as an easily understood form of good measurement for those of you who require a corroborating "fix."

The current rate of inflation is a unit of measurement you'll have no problem relating to. If your investments as a whole, including the new capital you've put in, are at least meeting that figure (after current taxes have been paid), you'll have met your minimal goal of staying even and maintaining your purchasing power. Better yet, you should try to exceed the annual inflation rate by at least 1 to 2 percent. If inflation is at 13 percent, "all" you need to do is have your investments return a net average of 13 to 15 percent (not easily accomplished when you also include the investment performance of your emergency funds, etc.). If the inflation rate changes, as it has and will, you shouldn't feel pressured to maintain that high level of performance: since the current annual inflation rate has dropped to approximately 4 percent, a 6 percent net return is still a good goal. And if you happen to be able to return a net 9 percent, so much the better. Falling interest rates, taken out of context, will absolutely put you on the money-go-round.

It's a simple rule of thumb, but it works. You'll attain financial security by consistently adding to and increasing your reserve purchasing power over a period of time. And if you can reinvest your investment capital and its profits, then do that too! If your investment assets can maintain that net 2 percent margin, the mathematics of compounding transform your investment into a spectacular gain and a greater assurance of attaining financial security. In five years, your investments and the new capital you've added would exceed the rate of inflation by 9.8 percent. That number would grow to 20.6 percent in 10 years, 45.3 percent in 20 years, and a very handsome 59 percent in 25 years. On a year-by-year basis it may not sound like much, but that 2 percent can indeed amount to a great deal over the longer term.

Now, if you add the rate of inflation to these figures, and add more time, the total return can be astounding. Dreyfus Fund, a large, conservative, growth-oriented mutual fund, proudly points to a gain of more than 3,800 percent since 1951. In the 33 years covered, the fund's average annual return was but 11.8 percent. Certainly respectable, but not what you'd expect from a 3,800 percent increase. Again, it demonstrates the mathematics of compounding.

If you can view the long term as a series of successful short-term solutions measured by your current goals and the current rate of inflation, you'll find the money-go-round becomes someone else's problem. When that person gets frustrated because his or her money market fund used to pay 15 percent, and now he or she cannot find an alternative investment paying a similar rate with comparable safety, you now know that person was losing money on an after-tax basis when inflation was at 13 percent and is making money today while inflation remains low. You'll also know that person probably failed to take into account total after-tax investment performance and failed to include new cash.

Once you have established a general objective with measurable goals, and also a method for measuring investment performance toward those goals, you're on your way. And don't let unexpected aberrations deter you. You may have a major emergency expense, or a lower-than-planned-for savings contribution. Just do the best you can. On the positive side, unexpected windfalls, a higher rate of return on your investment portfolio, or a salary increase might occur and that will help you make up for lost time without feeling forced to take that extra risk.

You still have major decisions ahead: where in particular to invest. There are two basic choices: debt-based assets and equity-based assets.

With debt-based assets, you, in effect, become a money lender. You have a contract under which the borrower agrees to pay interest regularly and repays the original sum at maturity. When interest rates go up, the market value of that contract will go down, and vice versa. If the debt asset is long term (a 30-year issue, for example) its market value can fluctuate more than ten times as much as a short-term asset.

When you purchase any long-term debt-based asset, consequently, you're inviting trouble if interest rates increase and you want to sell your holding before it matures. However, if you don't think you'll ever need to sell before maturity, then you may not care. A client of mine was once called by a newspaper reporter to "tell the world" how he felt about his $1 million municipal bond portfolio dropping more than 25 percent in value since interest rates were (then) so high. He responded, "Is that a fact! Well, I hadn't noticed. After all, they keep paying like clockwork."

For most clients, I recommend debt-based assets that mature in no more than 3 to 10 years, which is considered intermediate term. A longer maturity may give you a small amount of additional income, but what if you're forced to sell the asset in those extra years when interest rates have gone up, and the price of your asset, earning a lower rate, has fallen? The experts have enough trouble predicting interest rates in just six months time, so how can you be sure that interest rates will be the same, or lower, 20 years from now as they are today? And 20 years is a long, long time to wait unless you are prepared to sell your holdings at a possible loss in the interim.

The great speculator, Jesse Livermore, said it best, "I believe it is a safe bet that the money lost in (short-term) speculation is small compared with the gigantic sums lost by so-called (long-term) investors. Don't get rooted in long-term investments." Betting on tomorrow is chancy enough: betting on a day in the distant future is crazy.

Equity-based assets, by contrast, represent ownership. The most common of these assets is stock in companies, but they also encompass real estate, precious metals, agriculture, oil, and other investments. No return is promised on these assets, so their market value generally fluctuates over a much greater range than debt-based assets. That means this sort of investment gives a much greater potential for appreciation or loss.

Each of you, of course, has your own thoughts on how you can best use debt-based and equity-based assets. While I cannot give you the precise recommendations, since you have differing needs, desires, and comfort levels, I will provide you with a common-sense track to run on.

How should you allocate your new and existing investments between equity-based and debt-based assets? Answer: My earlier "words of general wisdom" — probably based on your age. The older you are, the less time you have to make up for investments that might reduce, forever, your overall performance. We both know you feel you can't afford to lose what you have. So if you're only five years away from retirement, it is more than likely that most of your portfolio will be in conservative debt-based assets.

Not long ago I had the privilege of reviewing President Reagan's 1984 federal income tax return for *Money Magazine*. And I noted that the president is just like the rest of us. As we get older, we become more conservative: we get "creeping conservatism." He has now sold all his investment real estate and taken back notes. The rest of his investment assets are made up of conservative stocks, bonds and Treasuries. "It's classic!" I told the magazine.

If your work life can still be measured in decades, on the other hand, and your chart of goals requires a legal-sized tablet, you will probably have the greatest concentration in equity-based assets. You'll discover that if you take some time to establish your measurable goals, miracles can happen. You will "instinctively" put in place a comfortable and appropriate mix of debt-based and equity-based assets, depending on your age. You will do so because you're naturally seeking your individual comfort level. For some of you, it may be 50 percent equity and 50 percent debt; for others, 80 percent equity and 20 percent debt. At the risk of repeating myself, if you decide what mix you need, based on measurable goals, you cannot make a serious mistake.

There are four other factors besides your age that you should consider when establishing your personal investment program: diversification, liquidity, taxes, and risk. As a financial professional, I consider each of these elements to be enormously important, but I know in the real world it's difficult to achieve a proper balance among them. If you leave out one element, or have an otherwise unbalanced combination, you will probably incur a serious problem. That's not the end of the world, of course, but you have created an unnecessary risk.

Diversification is perhaps the most frequently ignored principle of investing. Too often, due to lack of time or knowledge, or because of overconfidence or paralyzing anxiety, you will keep a vast proportion of your money in the bank, real estate, stocks, or your own business. And the result is that you are very vulnerable to the vicissitudes of one particular market.

Investment diversification solves that problem. A young couple whose major asset is a house, for example, should probably not buy additional real estate. They could consider, for example, an investment in the stock market. Executives who own a big block of stock in their company, for another example, should probably steer clear of the stock market. They could consider a portfolio of municipal bonds.

I've seen many times what a lack of diversification can do. A few years ago a man came to my office to discuss his situation, and it wasn't good. He was an officer of a Fortune 500 publicly held company and had been investing in the company's stock for 30 years. More than 80 percent of his net worth was tied to the fortunes of his employer, whom he obviously believed in, and he had refused to diversify though people had been telling him to for years. And for many years he was correct: the value of his stock continued to rise, as did the dividends.

Now, however, this man was retired, and his company had run into a severe cash squeeze. It had suspended its dividend, and the value of its stock has dropped dramatically. This former officer was forced to sell shares to "enjoy" his retirement years. The lesson is clear: if you decide to place all your eggs in one basket, you had better be willing to watch that basket very closely, or you had better be willing (and able) to make up for potentially large losses and to learn to enjoy egg on your face.

If you have concentrated your holdings in the mythical "safe" investment of an insured bank account or government bonds, you are taking an even greater risk today than in the past. It's not that the payor can't pay the interest and principal when due, but there's a greater risk today that the after-tax result will not keep pace with your purchasing power needs. The interest paid by banks and the government typically lags behind the rate of inflation. Once you take into account the income tax you'll have to pay on your gain, you will almost invariably fall seriously behind. Recent history demonstrates that times are becoming more volatile and that the peaks and valleys are becoming more pronounced — the highs higher and lows lower. A sudden burst of inflation and you will again find a wide gap between the interest you receive and the amount you need.

I believe a new notion of capital preservation is emerging, and its central credo is diversificatiion. It is now riskier not to diversify than to diversify. But don't go overboard: there's no sense in having your money in 40 different places. It's better to pick five or six sensible asset areas.

Let me back up for a moment and add some perspective about why you need to diversify. In the past couple of decades, inflation has shown a lot of volatility. Its upward movement has had a hand in increasing the value of the dollar, precious metals, real estate, oil, the stock market, and more. In just the past couple of years, however, we have seen a quick drop in inflation and interest rates, a falloff in the value of precious metals, oil, farmland, and many collectibles, and isolated movements in the stock market and real estate in general. A rise in interest rates is great for new bond issues, difficult for old ones, and hurts real estate and business expansion. A rise in bad news, on the other hand, causes precious metals, art, diamonds, and collectibles to rise but hurts the stock market. Unpredictable changes in the tax laws hurt everyone, and over the last nine years we have had five major changes, with a sixth coming.

What does all this mean? That we are all subject to terrible economic vicissitudes that none of us — none of us, I repeat — can control or predict (not even a good guess). But that does not mean we are helpless: it means that we have a limited range of options, and that within that range it's important to make good decisions. Thus we need goals to keep us on track and diversification to spread our risks. Simple, yes?

Rather than reacting to events, we need to plan ahead and follow basic economic principles. In September 1982, after the stock market had begun its dramatic rise, a television reporter called to ask me whether I was now directing clients toward the market. I answered that we already had money there.

Liquidity — the ability to convert your assets into cash without significant loss — is another investment consideration. A checking account at a bank can be very liquid, since automatic teller machines can supply cash 24 hours a day. An apartment building, however, is usually illiquid, for it can take many months to sell. To ensure at least minimum liquidity, I suggest you open (or maintain) a money-market mutual fund or a money-market insured deposit account, or a tax-free money-market account, if that is best for your tax bracket. Such accounts are easily accessible during emergencies, yet pay a market rate of interest. You can also consider as part of your liquid emergency funds your checking account, U.S. savings bonds, cash value on life insurance policies, and stocks. To further ensure your liquidity you could even open a line of credit at a bank or include the cash available through your credit cards. Still, I suspect that most of you will feel the best place to put your ready cash or assets is in some kind of money-market fund.

Some financial advisors say that the proper amount of liquid assets is three month's living expenses, perhaps six months if only one spouse is working. Each of my clients, however, is comfortable with a different level of liquidity — some at $250,000, others at $1,000. Either level, or anything in between or above or below, is acceptable — whatever makes you feel comfortable is what you should keep in liquid assets.

Remember that you can't look at liquidity in a vacuum. Before determining your comfort level, you need to examine your entire portfolio. How much of your assets can you readily liquidate if your goals change? If you get divorced? If one of your children needs money for a downpayment on a home? Common sense should prevail, as long as you think about it. If you are not sure of your job security or are in a volatile profession like advertising, you should probably have extra reserves. One client in such an occupation told me that if it weren't for those extra reserves, the between-jobs pressure she suffered would have been devastating. She was very thankful.

Taxes and their relationship to investments are always major considerations, since all investments must be considered on an aftertax basis. I will cover taxes in detail in chapter 13. Stay tuned.

Risk is perhaps the most important consideration of all. Why? Because the return on an investment generally increases very directly with the risk taken. Investments, by their nature, involve some level of risk, for otherwise there would be no return. Growth, for example, is just a probability game. To grow you have to have a lot of attempts, a portion of which will be failures. If you try to escape failures, you won't have successes. You never learn from success. Balancing your risks, then, is at the core of an investment philosophy. If the risky investments don't pay off, the slow and steady ones will keep you from being totally wiped out. Unfortunately, risk is a tricky factor, because the true risk of an investment is often difficult to assess and because most people have trouble assessing their taste for risk.

Every investment entails some risk. But you really don't have to measure that risk very accurately, if at all: it's more important that you know your own risk tolerance, your comfort level in trading the known for the unknown. Can you sleep at night once you've made a decision?

Risk doesn't only mean losing money or the value of an asset. There is also risk in being out of step with inflation — that is, not keeping up with it — in not performing well during deflation, and in losing sleep over your investment purchases. And there's the risk that you can't get out of your holdings when you need cash quickly. Remember, almost anything is easier to get into than out of. And there's the risk that the IRS or Congress will affect you adversely by disallowing a current tax advantage or changing a tax law.

There is no possible way, in short, that you or anyone else can begin to take all risks into account. I propose two rules of thumb. If there's a hint that the investment is riskless, RUN, don't walk away, or hang up the phone immediately and call the Better Business Bureau. The second rule is my "blink" test. If you blink after the risk is explained to you, you know you've exceeded your tolerance level.

• PART IV •

Keeping and Growing

Chapter 8

INVESTING FOR SAFETY

Most of you don't have much interest in interest rates except when you're buying a house or a car or looking for a good place to invest extra cash. Interest is interesting, but it can also be confusing. Even sophisticated people confuse debt instruments that bear interest with certain equity instruments that pay dividends. It is equity that produces real growth, and I'll discuss it in the next chapter: here we're talking about interest where investing money to earn interest is oriented not toward growth but toward safety.

Interest-bearing investments are the most basic element of a financial plan because they are both secure and productive. What's more, most people seem to like an investment that pays income, whether from interest or dividends. That regular check somehow makes an asset feel like a real investment. Pure growth just doesn't have the same psychological impact.

Though I have not attempted to make a formal study of this "fact," I think it's important to consider this thought before you invest. If only nonincome-paying potential growth investments are on your shopping list, you might be well advised to add an investment that pays interest (or a dividend) to your portfolio. Even if you don't require current income, that occasional check will possibly help you feel better about your investments. As a matter of fact, high-yield, low-risk investments should be considered the foundation of any well-designed investment strategy.

Let's look at some of the more common interest-bearing investment opportunities that offer relative safety.

PASSBOOK MONEY

Banks call it "dumb money," and they love it. Dumb money is a deposit that earns little or no interest but that the bank and savings and loan institutions can lend for maximum profit.

On March 31, 1986, the federal government will end the 5 1/2 percent interest-rate ceiling on passbook savings accounts, freeing banks and thrifts to pay any rate they wish on this $290 billion pool of funds. It is unlikely, however, that the rate will change much, and it is also unlikely that many people will change accounts.

Why? Most people are inert; they want to go through life unhassled. According to the bankers, passbook and statement savers generally are conservative, blue-collar, elderly, and prefer liquidity and an actual passbook they can see and clutch. According to the Federal Reserve Board, about 90 percent of savings accounts have balances of $1,000 or more. It isn't unusual for new clients to walk into my office with a number of passbook accounts, each holding $100,000.

Judy G. Barber of San Francisco is an expert in what she calls the psychology of money. Barber says that the people who leave substantial amounts of money in passbook accounts generally fit one of two profiles.

The first type of person, the most common, is a product of the depression. These people are highly conservative, she says, because those lean, often jobless, years taught them that frugality was a necessity. Security, more than additional income, is their primary concern. Even though the money-market accounts at banks and savings and loans are insured, these people are still wary of them. And this wariness about money is sometimes passed on to the next generation.

The second profile group is similar to the depression-era individual. These people either grew up in families where a great deal of money was lost or have themselves experienced major fluctuations in income. For these people, too, absolute security is more important than an increase in income.

If you see yourself in either of these groups, take note of it. You needn't change — chances are you couldn't in any significant way, even if you wanted to — but you should recognize why you do what you do. Once you've gotten that far, you may see the logic in earning more from your money for the same amount of risk, and may feel more comfortable shifting money from a passbook to a higher-paying certificate of deposit.

BANK MARKET-RATE AND SUPER-NOW ACCOUNTS

My favorite bank or savings and loan account is the market-rate or Super-NOW (Negotiable Order of Withdrawal) account because these accounts are liquid and have check-writing privileges. The market-rate account, as its name implies, pays market rates and is less flexible than the Super-NOW because you are limited in the number of checks you can write each month. The Super-NOW pays a slightly lower rate, offers greater flexibility, and like the market-rate account is insured to $100,000 by the Federal Deposit Insurance Corporation (FDIC). These are good accounts to have because they are more convenient than passbook savings, offer higher yields, and are also more liquid than certificates of deposits.

CERTIFICATES OF DEPOSIT (CDs)

These are the familiar time-deposit accounts offered by banks, thrifts, and now brokerage firms. With CDs, you lock up your money for a fixed amount of time, usually less than five years but longer if you like. The six-month period is the most popular. The longer the term, the higher the rate, obviously, but I would not suggest buying a CD with a maturity of more than five years if there is a possibility you may need your cash sooner. This is because all CD penalty provisions are stiff if you have to sell prematurely. If your funds are adequate, you might try buying sequential CD's, timing them so that one comes due each year for five years. If you don't need the money from the maturing CD, you could then purchase the next longest maturity. Since CDs of up to $100,000 are insured by the FDIC or the Federal Savings and Loan Insurance Corporation (FSLIC), they're perfectly safe; your money will be there when you go to get it.

The drawbacks? First, CDs are subject to early-withdrawal penalties, as mentioned above, usually at least 30 days' interest. Also, unless the

CD is part of an IRA or Keogh account or is in a trust for your child, you'll be fully taxed on the interest, though there are some CDs in which the interest (and tax) can be deferred for a year. However, CDs remain an excellent choice if you're in a relatively low tax bracket or you're looking for a way to save for a child's education. Since interest rates vary from bank to bank, as do minimum investment requirements, shop around a bit. Many of the publications mentioned earlier list the best CD rates offered throughout the country.

Wasn't life simple a few years back? Your choice in savings accounts amounted to two: passbooks or CDs. Now if you ask "What do you have?" be prepared to spend an hour.

U.S. TREASURY ISSUES

Backed by Uncle Sam, these are among the safest investments you can make. And they are exempt from state and local taxes, too, but not federal.

Treasury bills, maturing in 3, 6, or 12 months, are the shortest-term U.S. Treasury issues. They are sold in increments of $5,000, beginning with a $10,000 minimum purchase. They are issued in bearer form, not registered on the books of the issuer, and thus are payable to whoever possesses them; they should therefore be kept in a safe place. They are issued on a discount basis, which means they are sold below their face value — which is the amount you'll receive when the bill becomes due.

This last feature can be enormously important if you have received or will receive a lump sum of money and don't know what to do with it. If you purchase a Treasury bill that comes due next year, none of the interest will be taxed until the bill matures. This example illustrates beautifully what Treasury bills can be best at — safely storing funds while you figure out how to put them to their best use.

Treasury bills, and all other Treasury issues, can be purchased from banks or brokers or from Federal Reserve Banks when first issued. You can also purchase them as part of a U.S. government money-market fund, which I'll discuss later in this chapter.

Treasury notes are not discounted and pay interest at fixed rates every six months. The rate, of course, depends on maturity, which is from one to five years. For Treasury notes of two, three, and four years, the minimum purchase price is $5,000 and increases in multiples of $1,000. For notes over four years, the minimum purchase is only $1,000, which means that more people can afford them.

Many people buy Treasury *bills* but never consider Treasury *notes* or *bonds*. I think it's because people just aren't sure of the distinctions among bills, notes, and bonds. Also, Treasury bills are well publicized, but I bet if I asked 100 sophisticated investors the differences among Treasury bills, notes, and bonds, 80 couldn't explain the difference.

Treasury bonds make up most of the federal debt because the government finances primarily for the long term. These instruments can be intermediate term — 5 to 10 years — or long-term — up to 30 years — and are available in units of $1,000 to $10,000 in both registered (with your name on it) and bearer form. Interest is paid semiannually, as with Treasury notes.

Treasury notes and bonds are essentially the same, the primary difference being the length of maturity.

I believe both these notes and bonds can have a place in your portfolio, for the same reason a CD can. The bearer feature of Treasury bonds may be of special interest to some of you, but the high safety feature should be of interest to all. If the FDIC had to step in to protect your CD, there might be some delay in payment and uneasiness on your part. That will not happen with Treasury issues.

Zero-coupon bonds are relatively new but are fast becoming a staple of both the small and large investor's portfolio. They are simple, inexpensive, and particularly attractive as investment vehicles for IRAs, Keoghs, self-directed retirement plans, and college education plans.

These investments have an unusual way of getting to your portfolio. After buying Treasury bonds or notes, brokerage firms strip them of their interest coupons, rechristen them zero-coupon bonds, and resell them to investors at well below their face value. When the zero matures, all principal and interest is paid to the investor. Because a zero retains its interest payments and reinvests them at the same rate, this is the only interest-bearing investment in which you know what you'll end up with before you put down your money.

The awful twist is that the income from a zero is taxable *now*, even though you won't see a penny of it until the bond or note matures. That is why zeros are so appealing for qualified retirement plans or trusts for your children. In a retirement plan the tax on the income is deferred until you withdraw money, and if in trust for a child, the tax will occur in that child's low (or no) tax bracket.

Corporations and municipalities also offer zero-coupon bonds. But for maximum safety, U.S. Treasury zeros can't be beat. In fact, if you have limited cash, are in a low tax bracket, and need to earn a specific amount for a future debt, zero-coupon bonds may be one of the better ideas around.

I think it's important to point out, however, that the market values of zeros will fluctuate much more than a comparable yielding and maturing Treasury bond that actually pays out income. Like other bonds, zero-coupon bonds are bought with the idea that interest rates won't go up. Because zeros don't pay interest or principal until maturity, if prevailing interest rates rise, the value of the bonds will decline more than the value of conventional bonds. A 10-year zero is nearly twice as volatile in price as a 10-year conventional bond; a 20-year zero is about three times as risky as a 20-year conventional, and a 30-year zero is about four times as risky as a bond of the same maturity. Moral of the story: If you think you might have to sell your zero before maturity, don't buy them in the first place.

Now let's test your investment knowledge of another government debt instrument. Can you name an investment that involves no commission or fee, is totally secure, has no risk of principal loss, provides the option to postpone federal tax liability until redemption, is free from state and local taxes, has a guaranteed minimum interest rate of $7^1/_2$ percent, a variable yield compounded semiannually, and a minimum investment requirement of only $25?

No guesses? Well, prepare to be surprised: it's a *U.S. savings bond.* But, you ask, "Aren't you supposed to buy U.S. savings bonds only if you're feeling particularly patriotic; are 'requested' to do so by your boss; or can't think of a better gift for a birthday, Christmas, or bar mitzvah?" Answer: Not any longer. The ugly duckling is now a lovely swan.

Everyone thinks they know everything there is to know about savings bonds. After all, most of us have owned a few at one time or another. Perhaps you still have some in your safe-deposit box from years ago. Take note: If "years ago" is more than 40, the bonds don't pay interest anymore and can no longer be used to defer taxes.

Today, you can buy what is now called an EE bond for as little as $50 or as much as $10,000 in face value. Its face value is *always* twice the purchase price, reflecting the fact that you will receive your interest in a lump sum, along with your original investment when you redeem the bond. In order to qualify for the variable rate, however, EEs must be held five years. That feature almost makes them seem like zero-coupon bonds, but there's a significant difference: the tax deferral available with the U.S. savings bond gives them an advantage over zeros if used outside of retirement plans or trusts. As I noted above, you have to pay income tax on the deferred interest on a zero-coupon bond each year even though it isn't received, but the tax due on a EE savings bond is automatically deferred.

I believe the variable rate of interest on EEs gives them another advantage over zero-coupon bonds. When inflation rises, interest rates usually follow. With EE's variable rate, you won't get out of step with the times. This floating rate is reset every May and November at 85 percent of the average market yield on five-year Treasury notes and bonds sold during the previous six months, but as I stated earlier, the rate is guaranteed not to fall below $7\frac{1}{2}$ percent, even if 85 percent of the prevailing Treasury yields would theoretically drop the rate below that figure. That's *especially* attractive if interest rates continue to drop, and in addition, there's no cap on how high the rate can go.

Now you can have your cake and eat it too. But remember, it wasn't always this good. Just a few years ago, these bonds (then called Es not EEs) paid a maximum fixed interest rate of $8\frac{1}{2}$ percent at a time when you could earn 15 percent elsewhere. Now, with an unlimited upside and a fixed downside, there aren't very many high-yielding investments that can compete. Why, then, hasn't your favorite advisor told you about EEs? You guessed it . . . no commission.

Unfortunately, EEs still have an image problem. One of my clients, a military officer, was quite embarrassed when he told me he had a lot of his money in U.S. savings bonds. Embarrassed because he "knew" it wasn't a good investment. But he was also proud to be putting his money and faith in his country. That feeling of comfort, I must stress again, can be more important that the investment itself, which in this case happens to be a good one. Investing in savings bonds was indeed best for him.

Series HH bonds, available only through an exchange of at least $500 in Series E or EE bonds, pay a fixed annual $7 \frac{1}{2}$ percent interest rate. Their advantage is that you can exchange Es and EEs into HHs without incurring a tax liability. You would do so, presumably, because you now desire to receive a check and because continued safety is assured. HHs can be an excellent vehicle for some of your retirement funds.

Federal agency securities are similar to the government securities discussed above, but they usually produce a slightly higher rate of return. All kinds of agencies offer instruments, from Banks for Cooperatives to the Small Business Administration, from Federal International Credit Banks to the U.S. Postal Service. Agency securities come in so many shapes and sizes, you really need an expert — probably your broker — to help determine which of these instruments, if any, would best suit your needs. With the exception of Ginnie Maes, my guess is that most of these securities will simply confuse you — unless you like to stay up all night studying them.

Ginnie Mae pass-throughs (Ginnie Mae's short for GNMA, the Government National Mortgage Association) are the best known in this group. Backed by a pool of Federal Home Administration and Veterans Administration residential mortgages, they are available for a cash payment of $25,000 or through shares of various mutual funds or unit trusts (explained later in this chapter). They are called pass-throughs because that's what they do — pass through interest and principal payments to the security holder in monthly checks. Ginnie Mae guarantees that investors will receive timely principal and interest payments even if homeowners do not make mortgage payments on time. Since most home mortgages are repaid or refinanced, on the average, in 12 years, the income from a Ginnie Mae security will decline after that time period.

Ginnie Maes are popular and I like them. I like the fact that they are high-yielding, intermediate term, and self-liquidating. They are excellent for retirees. For those of you who don't need the income now, you can take advantage of a Ginnie Mae mutual funds' automatic reinvestment program and gain the benefits of compounding. Ginnie Mae funds (available only through securities dealers) are particularly good for IRAs because they are safe and more convenient than CDs, since all your money stays in one place. With CDs, you'll have a new maturity date and a new investment each year. In 20 years you'll have 20 of them, and who wants to deal with that?

TAX-EXEMPT BONDS

Everyone wants to decrease his or her tax payments. Since municipal bonds offer interest with no federal tax — and no state and local taxes, if issued in your state of residence — it's small wonder that these bonds are one of the more popular investments today. To determine whether you should purchase a taxable or a tax-free bond you need to calculate the equivalent taxable yield for a tax-free bond. You make the conversion by dividing the return rate of the tax-exempt bond by the reciprocal of your tax bracket (the reciprocal is 100 minus your tax rate — 51 percent if your bracket is 49 percent, 60 percent if your bracket is 40 percent, etc.). So if the tax-free bond pays 6 percent, and your tax bracket is 42 percent, divide 6 by 58 percent, or 0.58. The equivalent taxable yield for this 6 percent tax-free bond, consequently, is 10.34 percent. This and other formulas can help you calculate the advantages of owning either tax-free or taxable bonds, but generally, if you're in a federal tax bracket of at least 35 percent, you should consider municipal bonds.

Municipals currently are issued in registered form, but most outstanding issues are in bearer form. The bearer form is popular with many clients simply because of its anonymity. Interest is paid in six-month intervals for both forms, but paid directly to holders of registered bonds, while those who own bearer bonds must clip their coupons and personally redeem them for cash.

One of the unusual features of municipal bonds is their wide range of available maturity dates. When issued, the bonds' maturities usually go from 1 to 30 years, and municipalities often offer bonds that mature in each of these years. This makes a municipal bond investment an excellent candidate for establishing a sequential maturity portfolio, which may reduce the risk of changing interest rates. Since the longest-term bonds pay the best yield, however, most investors continue to prefer bonds with the longest maturities. As I've mentioned more than once, that's a dangerous gamble.

Tax-exempt bonds are one of the most valuable tools for personal financial planning. No tricks, no gimmicks, and best of all, no income tax. But they should be used judiciously, as part of your plan, not as the sole solution.

For the first-time municipal bond buyer purchasing individual bonds, I generally advocate purchasing only insured or top-quality, triple-A-rated bonds. Insured bonds guarantee that principal and interest payments will be made; about one-quarter of the municipals issued in 1984 were insured by independent insurance companies.

If you already hold individual municipal bonds that are only rated "A," you shouldn't feel you have to sell. Even if your bonds have less than an "A" rating, the odds are still very much with you. Fewer than 1 percent of *all* municipal bonds issued since the depression have gone into default, and an even smaller percentage never repaid their obligations.

There are so many different types of municipal bonds available, and so many nuances to consider that whole books have been devoted to these bonds. You almost need a computer to keep track of all the variables. If you don't wish to get caught up in the details of municipal bonds; if you don't understand, or don't want to understand, things like call features or the difference between general obligation and revenue bonds, buy shares in a tax-exempt bond fund. In this type of fund, you have good diversification, better liquidity than with a single bond, and active management.

You can also achieve diversification through *unit-investment trusts.* These trusts are, in this instance, groups of tax-exempt bonds put together in one portfolio, with pieces of the total package then sold to individual investors. They usually are not professionally managed, however, and their values are difficult to locate, which is why I prefer municipal bond mutual funds. Since mutual funds can play such an important role in your financial plan, I discuss them in greater depth in chapter 12. However, whichever vehicle you choose, I continue to recommend avoiding long-term portfolios.

TAX-DEFERRED ANNUITIES

Tax-deferred annuities are another way to lessen the tax bite on your interest. They aren't tax free, of course, like tax-exempt bonds, but the tax on interest is deferred until you withdraw income. If you're in the 50 percent tax bracket, your tax-deferred money could double in an annuity in half the time it takes the same amount of fully taxed money to double. Those in a lower tax bracket would still find an annuity highly advantageous.

I like tax-deferred annuities. They are contracts between you and a life insurance company, which are available through insurance companies and securities dealers. The company agrees to pay you a fixed amount of money each month, or at regular intervals, for the period of time you specify — often from age 65 until death. You may buy a contract with a single large premium or add to your investment by paying additional premiums.

They are tailor-made investments for people placing money aside for retirement because the tax-deferral feature is the key to this investment. The principal is usually guaranteed, even if you take your money out the day after you've put it in. And the current income rate is generally guaranteed for three months, six months, one year, or three years. Some insurance companies guarantee the current rate for as long as five years. Most plans tie the nonguaranteed interest rates that follow to some sort of price index, thus allowing the annuity to remain competitive with other interest-bearing investments.

Though you may not know much about deferred annuities, the concept is not new. As a matter of fact, they date back to the Roman Empire. What you need to remember, however, is that they are a complex vehicle, just like municipal bonds. There is much you can learn; partial surrender charges, ways to rate the companies that guarantee the contracts, the various types of annuities, their payout options, and so on. You won't get caught up on the money-go-round by such details if you observe a few basic rules.

Look for an "escape" or "bailout" clause. Some annuities allow you to take out all of your money at no charge if interest rates fall more than 1 or 2 percent below the rate at the time of purchase. Look for a similar bailout clause if the renewal rate for your annuity lags more than 1 or 2 percent behind the rates of the insurance company's new annuity offerings.

The second basic rule is simply making sure that you only consider annuities offered by companies rated "A" or better by A.M. Best Co., an independent insurance analyst. The Lipper Analytical Survey will also help you determine which companies have been (and currently are) doing well.

If you are concerned about possible changes in tax law (see chapter 14) where some sort of modified flat or fair tax is approved by Congress and deferred-annuity income becomes taxable, not to worry — it'll probably affect only future investments. Anyway, I believe existing annuity programs will likely be "grandfathered."

If you do nothing until you're absolutely certain about where the tax laws are going, that's fine. I believe that while you could lose certain benefits from a new investment because of tax law changes, you will also gain from the existing benefits in the interim. Until the tax-deferral feature is rejected (if ever), the deferred portion of your annuity will accumulate; after such a law is passed, you will be taxed at a lower rate. And as I noted above, it's likely that current investments will be grandfathered.

CORPORATE BONDS

Another kind of vehicle you should consider is the *corporate bond.* And as you can probably guess, I'm going to tell you there are more types of corporate debt instruments (from equipment trust certificates, to convertible bonds, to Eurobonds), and strategies where they can be applied, than you'll ever know what to do with. There's something for everyone, that's for sure — even maturities exceeding 100 years. The only thing to be aware of is that in general a corporate bond is likely to be riskier than the government debt instruments previously mentioned because the risk of default by a corporation is usually greater than that of a government. Since a corporate bond's safety is generally accounted for in the bond's rating, I usually recommend a AA or AAA rating and maturity dates that do not exceed the intermediate term (3 to 10 years) to reduce change of rating risk and interest rate risk.

Like municipal bonds, corporate bonds can be purchased individually, through mutual funds, or through unit trusts. Once again, I prefer the mutual fund purchase. Corporate bonds can also be purchased through "closed-end" funds, where a fixed number of shares are outstanding and are traded and valued on the open market. ("Open-end" mutual funds are where you buy from and sell your shares directly to the management company at a net asset value.)

PRIVATE LOANS

Though these "investments" are of lower security, I can't overlook *private personal loans*. People frequently loan significant sums of money to friends or members of the family, and I'm afraid these loans often cause trouble. Most such loans are made because you know the borrower, not because it's a good investment. When push comes to shove, will you really be able to foreclose, even if the loan is secured? If you do make personal loans, I believe you should view the money as possibly noncollectible funds. Any other view is likely to "teach you a lesson" you'd prefer not to learn.

DIVIDEND-PAYING STOCKS

I'm going to detour here for a moment to discuss cash dividends paid by common and preferred stocks, which also provide safety. I will provide a more complete description of these types of investments in the following chapter (I'm almost there), but here I merely wish to point out that paid dividends act, at times, like interest-bearing investments. As long as a stock pays a dividend, be it a utility or a corporate stock, there is a point below which the stock will not usually drop. Someone, somewhere will be interested in purchasing your holding, if only for the yield. Its relative yield will increase as the securities' market value falls. If the dividend is intact and secure, the lower security price will make its purchase more attractive. In short, it can work very much like a debt instrument.

I often recommend individual utility stocks (the exception to my "don't buy individual issues" rule) or utility mutual funds even if a client is not particularly enamored of the stock market. Utility stocks can behave like bonds, but if you own utilities, you can also participate in any dividend increase. Dividend-producing investments, whether directly or through mutual funds, can be another highly liquid, high-reward addition to a portfolio where income and safety are important.

MONEY MARKET FUNDS

You may well be wondering why I detoured into a discussion of dividends before I talked about *money market mutual funds.* Well, there's a simple reason: even if 100 percent of the income from a money market mutual fund is *interest,* the government still calls it a *dividend,* but the IRS won't allow you the dividend exclusion on this interest/dividend/whatever-you-want-to-call-it. Ah, yet another government sleight of hand.

A money market fund is a mutual fund that provides free checkwriting privileges and seeks maximum current interest through investments in specified money market instruments. The fund can invest in a diversified or undiversified group of high-yielding borrowings, such as CDs, Treasury securities, government agency issues, corporate promissory notes, and other obligations. All these instruments have short maturities, sometimes averaging as little as one day. When short-term investments earn high interest rates, money market fund rates can be higher than those of savings accounts or certificates of deposit.

I'm frequently asked about the safety of money market funds. And this is a consideration, since banks and savings and loans accounts are insured up to $100,000 and the money market funds do not have such insurance. In my opinion, these funds are still very low risk. They select short-term investments of low-risk issuers, and would incur losses only if these major issuers defaulted on their obligations. And even that would involve but a small portion of the portfolio. The other noteworthy risk, that of the fund management company having financial problems, is negligible if you select a recognized major money market fund.

If you're still a little leery of money funds, you can further increase the already high safety by investing in a fund that invests only in U.S. government obligations. Since this type of fund is low risk, the yields will be somewhat less than those of other money market funds. U.S.

government and regular money market funds can be purchased through securities dealers or by dealing directly with the management companies.

BANK MARKET-RATE ACCOUNTS
vs.
MONEY MARKET FUNDS

In 1982 deregulation of the banking industry enabled banks to market accounts that compete with money market funds. The banks' market-rate accounts initially paid higher rates than money market funds in an effort to regain the many billions of dollars that had earlier flowed out of the banking system and into the money funds. After that early period, bank rates fell and are still somewhat lower than money market fund rates.

The major competitive advantage of the banks' market-rate accounts is that they are insured by the FDIC. The competitive edge of the money funds comes in the form of lower minimum balances (bank account yields drop to passbook rates if the balance is below $2,500) and more flexible check-writing privileges (if you write more than three checks in any given statement month, bank account yields drop to passbook rates).

The Super-NOW account, your third choice, was introduced after the market-rate account. It requires a minimum balance of $2,000 and allows unlimited check-writing. It pays a yield approximately 1 percent below the market-rate account.

The proper choice for you among these three depends on your feelings about flexibility, safety, and yield. The money market mutual fund provides the best combination of yield and flexibility, but it is not insured. In order to be fully insured, you have to make some sacrifice in either flexibility or yield.

• Chapter 9

INVESTING IN REAL ESTATE

Debt instruments like passbook accounts and money market funds are typically the first place you put your money. But they don't have to be the *only* first place. If most of you have a financial choice, real estate would certainly be in the running as well.

The lure of real property is its tangibility. It's something you can see, touch, walk through, live in, or rent out. Another is its familiarity — most of you have bought or rented a single-family house or condominium. Historically, almost all types of real estate have been excellent hedges against inflation. And for some people real estate has provided enormous amounts of money. As a matter of fact, most of the great fortunes in the United States were created by real estate investment. Somehow it "feels" that when you own real estate, you can't lose. However, many of you have already discovered (or will soon discover) that real estate ownership is simply not automatically profitable. The "sure thing" is no more.

Now more than ever, the key to any investment success is value. And value, of course, is a function of supply and demand. Value, which in the boom years of real estate often took a back seat to dreams of huge profits, has reemerged as the undisputed, essential characteristic of any property. And value is value, no matter how the potential buyer assesses it: by conducting an in-depth computer analysis or by simply stepping back from a house or lot or apartment complex and asking, "How do I feel about this property?"

Don't scoff. Your gut (intuitional) feelings about the soundness of the deal when it's first presented should not be lightly dismissed, particularly when the seller wants your investment money yesterday. Sometimes the urgency is artificially created to prevent you from

seeing all the dimensions of a deal. As is true with all investment opportunities, if your intuition tells you no, then no it should be. A yes
shouldn't be a final commitment, either, but the crossing of a threshold. Now you move forward to investigate thoroughly all of the relevant factors that affect the deal: everything from the economics to the
safeguards, from the liability to the type of property. And all that takes
time.

There's no shortage of opportunities in real estate, but that could be
said of just about every type of investment. What is a bit different about
real estate is the time it takes to invest and the time you should expect
to hold it. Let me emphasize again that the vast majority of people who
have made sizable profits through investing in real estate were conservative people investing for the long term. They weren't looking for a
killing. Many of them just happened to be in the right place at the right
time — before the U.S. experienced double-digit inflation.

You're asking for trouble if you're counting on such high inflation to
again provide you with windfall profits. Over the years I have learned
that when investing, you have to have a lot of patience as well as a lot of
staying power. My clients who have made the most money through
real estate have learned that valuable lesson. Mistakes in real estate
can be especially disastrous because of the large amount of money
usually involved, but often, if you can afford to hold on, you'll find
things turn in your favor. Many investors — even successful ones, at
times — must sell their holdings because they are so heavily in debt
(overleveraged) they can't weather the bad times any other way.

Real estate, almost more than any other investment, can be charac-
terized by leverage. That is, borrowing money to buy what you want
with as little cash as possible. Unless there is a tax change, the great
advantage to investment real estate is that you can deduct more than
the amount invested without being liable to pay off the leverage. In a
real estate investment, you can sign nonrecourse notes and take the
resulting deductions for interest and depreciation — something you
cannot do with any other investment.

These deductions can help you create tax losses to shelter income
from other sources. And leverage is the important factor in creating
these losses, which come about, for example, because depreciation is
based on the gross purchase price and interest is charged against the

amount you owe. Your paper loss from depreciation may be greater than your payments, and the loss you finally calculate will probably be much greater than your initial cash investment. A substantial amount of the deduction will spill over into your other income. The more leverage used, the greater the paper "loss" and the better the opportunity for capital appreciation ... or real loss. If moderate leverage is used, the appreciation potential is less, but current income will often be created as well as a lower risk.

You can, of course, acquire real estate with no mortgage debt. Growth, after all, comes from property economics and not leverage. Here appreciation should equal or exceed the rate of inflation and the mostly sheltered income could approach 10 percent depending on the part of the country in which you invest. In these uncertain times, I recommend that you reduce your risk by reducing the capital you borrow and increasing your equity investment. A solid equity will mean lower break-even requirements and the ability to ride out occasional adverse fluctuations in income.

An alternative to holding substantial equity in property is to establish an appropriate reserve in a money-market account, or in government securities, as the downside buffer. These are uncertain times, and I believe that real estate investors may be poised at the edge of a no-win situation. If inflation remains down, for example, it may become a drag on real estate values. People have grown to expect quick appreciation from real estate, and if it doesn't happen, the market may become depressed. We're already seeing that in different parts of the country. And if inflation rates go up again, long-term credit might become harder to get because of the disastrous effects high inflation has on lenders, whether individuals, institutions, or the government. Today, with the higher risk associated with increased real estate uncertainty, portfolio diversification also becomes an even more important factor.

If you have some cash to risk and you find real estate appealing, you have two fundamental decisions to make. The first concerns your portfolio; what proportions of your discretionary income and savings, if any, should be in real property. The second is whether you wish to be a landlord or to invest in group ownership with professional management.

You have to come to grips with the idea of being a landlord. Do you want to be bothered with flooded basements, collapsing roofs, backed-up toilets (discovered at 2 A.M., of course), exploding boilers, litigious tenants . . . you know what it's like. Owning rental property directly can be just like owning a second business — very time-consuming.

Another possibility is to create a joint venture with one or more other investors. But this alternative also requires a substantial down-payment and limits your diversification. And initially it's just as much work: you still need to research, evaluate, and negotiate about the property, and then someone has to manage it.

If you have the expertise and time to pursue it, individual or joint ownership can be quite satisfactory. You have a lot of control over the property and its eventual sale, particularly if you're the sole owner. Most of the time, however, I do not recommend individual ownership, simply because most people don't have the time and/or expertise to make it a successful proposition.

Another way to invest in real estate is through a real estate syndication, also known as a limited partnership (see chapter 13). There are two types of limited partnerships: public and private. The typical investor in a publicly offered real estate limited partnership has an annual income of $45,000 to $60,000 per year and usually places between $8,000 to $11,000 in partnerships. In private placement limited partnerships (35 investors or less) suitable investor guidelines are far more restrictive, and investment minimums often start at $50,000 or $100,000. In both kinds of partnerships the managing partner pools the investors' money into a portfolio of properties, which are often diversified by geography and sometimes by type of real estate.

You can reduce or eliminate many of the risks and difficulties of real estate investing by taking care in choosing the specific syndication and matching the various real estate benefits with your investment objectives. If you are in a lower tax bracket, you might not be able to use the tax losses effectively. If you're a high-tax-bracket investor, you may prefer the advantages of a leveraged partnership. Again, you should think about your income, net worth, age, and future income sources and requirements (see chapter 6).

Public syndications in 1984 earned annual rates of return ranging from 12 percent to 16 percent or better, depending on the type of property. A return in this range is a good benchmark to aim for. Though syndicators may charge for their services as much as 25 percent of each dollar invested, 1984 average performance figures suggest that syndications are still very worthwhile.

Selecting a sponsor takes a lot of knowledge and understanding of the industry (see chapter 14). But there are a couple of questions you can ask that will help you separate possible good investments from the not so good. First, ask about the sponsor's projected holding period. I suggest it should be between five and seven years. Second, ask whether the sponsor has, in the past, usually sold properties for "paper" — that is, provided seller financing rather than negotiating for straight cash. The latter is better for the investor. If the sponsor takes paper — in effect, acts as a lender — your grandchildren may receive all the real investment rewards.

You may have heard that some real estate syndicators have pushed property values up to unrealistically high levels. I can attest to that. An apartment building was recently sold in Dallas for $2.1 million. The buyer put $100,000 down, but later purposely forfeited his deposit: he refused to close the deal because he became convinced he would later lose much more than $100,000. When I asked the seller what he was going to do now, he said he was going to put it back on the market for $4.3 million. "This way," he said, "someone will offer me half-price, and I'll get what I wanted in the first place." Two months later a syndicator paid $4.3 million for the property. I'm sure this is not a daily occurrence, but it can show the nature of the market.

Interestingly, syndicators do not represent as much of the market as commonly believed. A recent study of New York City indicated that only 8 percent of all real estate purchases in 1983 were made by syndications.

I believe that just about everyone should have some real estate in his or her portfolio. Even if you are retired, you can select conservative real estate investments that produce good income with low amounts of debt. These will still have some opportunity for growth. You shouldn't swear off growth opportunities forever, no matter what your age is. If real estate constitutes 25 to 35 percent of your investment worth in younger years, it can still constitute 5 to 10 percent in later years.

If individual, joint, or syndicate ownership is not to your liking, real estate investment trusts, or REITs, are yet another way for you to participate in a diversified portfolio of properties. You buy REIT shares — stocks traded on major stock exchanges — from a company that has purchased a variety of properties or loaned money to real estate developers. REITs are required by law to pay out 95 percent of their earnings on an annual basis, however, so your tax benefits are limited to the amount of the distribution. The shares offer both diversity and liquidity, and this last characteristic gives REITs an important advantage over limited partnerships — where you cannot sell your partnership shares at any time, you can sell your REIT shares.

At the moment, REITs are waging a tough battle with public syndicators over investor dollars. More REITs were registered or completed in the first quarter of 1985 than in all of 1984. And for good reason: there's a lot of investor confidence in the REIT market, and the IRS has made clear it is serious about going after syndicators who seem to be selling real estate as a tax shelter rather than as an investment. You can get into REITs for very little money: as little as $500 can bring you a percentage of a diversified group of properties across the country.

Still another real estate trust you may wish to consider is called a finite life real estate investment trust (FREIT). These investments are also an alternative to real estate limited partnerships, for they also either purchase properties (leveraged or unleveraged) or make mortgage loans. The FREIT, however, is scheduled to be liquidated within a designated time frame, whereas a limited partnership only suggests a time frame as a goal. One of the advantages the FREIT has over a partnership is the liquidity of the shares (also traded on an exchange) and their lower risk. The primary disadvantage is that FREITs also cannot pass through additional losses, only income.

If investment risk concerns you, I suggest you consider an income-oriented REIT, an all-cash FREIT, or an all-cash limited partnership. These entities pay cash for properties and so carry no debt, thus producing high income with low investment risk.

There is still one more real estate investment opportunity, however, of which most of you are probably unaware. It's a rather complex arrangement in which a real estate partnership purchases your limited-partnership interest. These real estate partnerships do just one thing: they acquire partnership units from investors who wish to cash out of their investments before they've gone full cycle and sold all their properties.

Publicly offered real estate limited partnerships, when new, have relatively high start-up costs, and that means the investor must hold it long enough to allow the properties' value to appreciate and overcome its initial expenses. If, however, you purchase a unit in a limited partnership that has purchased someone else's older partnership interest, much of the risk and upfront expense has already been dealt with. Although most older partnerships are sold as 7- to 10-year investments — because many partnerships take back a mortgage when a property is sold — the average life is in the 10- to 15-year range.

An investment in this sort of partnership, since some of the risk has been eliminated, is usually at the halfway mark in terms of performance. Many financial advisors can give you a prospectus that will tell you more about these partnerships and their minimum qualifications.

It would only confuse you if I began to detail and compare the merits (or demerits) of various types of real estate — shopping centers, apartment complexes, office buildings, industrial parks, miniwarehouses, agriculture, raw land, and the like. Nor would it help you get off the money-go-round if I set out to describe the "best" regions in the country in which to invest. Again, "best" depends on your goals. Each kind of investment and each geographical area carries a different objective and risk.

Just how much of your portfolio should be invested in real estate depends on the factors mentioned earlier but should also include personal concern about inflation and liquidity and whatever other issues you think are relevant. And if you decide against any form of real estate, don't worry, we'll still be friends.

• Chapter 10

INVESTING IN STOCKS

Almost all of us at one time or another have picked up the newspaper, turned to the business section, and read that day's stock market report. But how often has it occurred to you that most of the time no one has any idea why the market went up or down?

It's true.

A few years ago, a broker I knew at the New York Stock Exchange was asked by a television reporter why the market went down that day. The broker wasn't quite sure what to say, so he told the reporter that he would ask other professionals for their views before he went on the air. The best response the broker could get was, "Today, there were more sellers than buyers." The answer that ended up on television was different, of course, but you get the idea. There is a simple rationale to explain daily stock market activity, and people have spent their lives trying to figure out what it is. I sometimes think the stock market is like a bumblebee; it shouldn't be able to fly, but it does.

When you buy a stock you are buying equity in a company and its potential growth. You are investing directly in the economic system, sharing in both its risks and benefits. That seems very logical and straightforward, but in fact the stock market rarely is. It can be awfully frustrating when the company in which you've invested your hard-earned money shows a substantial increase in earnings, but the stock drops like a rock because the entire market declined due to lower-than-expected earnings at IBM or an "expert's" prediction that a market downturn was about to occur.

I'm convinced most people choose to buy individual stocks for one of four major reasons, or a combination of these reasons. They buy stocks because they find old habits difficult to break — their generation was taught to believe that people *had* to invest extra cash in the stock market. Another reason is that people want to do *something* besides sock their money away in a savings account, and individual stocks seem the easiest, most liquid, and most available alternative — perhaps the only one. A third reason is ego: Owning shares in a company can make a person not only feel good, but can also provide good country club or barber or beauty shop conversation. And lastly, individual stocks can be exciting: the thrill of "winning" money is more attractive than the boredom of *making* money.

I sincerely believe that over the long term, people who choose their own stocks (especially with the aid of a broker) rarely make money in the market. I tell that to everyone, whether the listener is a serious investor, casual investor, or trader. Though one person's investment history hardly constitutes a thorough study, let's look at the track record of an investor I know.

About three years ago, the president of a company listed on the New York Stock Exchange came into my office shaking his head. He had invested seriously in the stock market for 20 years, owning many individual issues and following them very closely. He had an accounting background, kept meticulous records, and was very confident of his performance — until someone challenged his results. The president, taking up the gauntlet, carefully reconstructed his stock market activity, noting additions of new capital and withdrawals of older capital. He also took into account all dividends received and taxes paid. After 20 years (from 1960 to 1980) he discovered he ended up only breaking even. He hadn't made any money! And if he had stopped in 1978, he would have been seriously behind . . . that's not even taking inflation into account! If *you* are a serious stock investor, you should check your long-term record as well. You too might be surprised.

Serious investors often belong to the first group I mentioned above — those who trade in the stock market because they "always have." Then there are those who see the stock market as their only alternative, which is frequently correct because they haven't got much motivation to look around. What happens? Usually, these people lose money, not understanding that an investment in individual stocks requires a great deal of time. In addition, the cost of buying and selling stocks, especially with a full service broker, is higher than many people realize. You have to have a 40-point rise in the Dow just to break even with a typical blue-chip stock. Thus, thinking of the market as just someplace to put their money, such people turn a potentially good investment into nothing more than a gamble, and a bad gamble at that. Sad, I know, but true. Unable to relate to the activities of the market and unwilling to research and follow the stocks they buy, these people might be better off investing their $500 in any kind of business in the neighborhood — at least then they might pay attention to the soundness and progress of their investment.

If an investor needs his or her ego massaged — our third group — the stock market can be the perfect place. The price may be unusually high, however, and the massage often leaves bruises. Besides, it's no fun to compare losers in the locker or powder room; chances are your ego will be rubbed the wrong way.

Lastly, there's the trader. I could never believe that traders make serious money. As a matter of fact, a recent study about securities trading has confirmed my impression. The researcher concluded that in all tax brackets, high appreciation is required to achieve even a modest return. Why? Because commissions add up very quickly, and because traders pay high taxes on their short-term capital gains. Even if Congress permitted investors to consider as a long-term holding anything they've owned more than one month, and so have their gain at sale taxed at a lower rate, the traders still probably wouldn't do well. According to this study, a trader, paying discount commissions and only 20 percent in taxes on long-term gains would still need an annual appreciation rate of 34.9 percent just to break even. While trading may be appropriate for short periods, only the most clairvoyant traders, obviously, will be able to accumulate wealth in the long run.

During my almost 20-year involvement with the stock market, the only people I know who have made significant amounts of money through individual stock ownership are those who owned private companies which favorably merged with public companies — or who had vast holdings in such a company before their company went public. They were then able to sell their below-market-cost shares for a very, very nice profit. If you do not wish to follow in their footsteps and you still want to end up with $1 million by purchasing individual stocks, just start with $4 million. If you don't have $4 million but only a small sum, you will at least gain some experience by investing in individual stocks — the experience of watching your broker significantly increase his or her commission sum while your small sum hardly increases at all

— if it doesn't go down. As a matter of fact, you'll hope you live long enough to use all the experience you've gained.

I won't even bother to comment on people trading options except to note that they are just as short-sighted as they are short-term. Trading options is pure gambling.

An eternal truth: Save time and emotional energy. Try to understand *why* you're putting money into the stock market. If you're in the market in a casual way, to have a little fun, play alongside the big wheels — maybe you'll get lucky, it's fine, if that's what you want to do. But if you're serious about providing for your future security, about attempting to achieve your goals, then do what the president of the N.Y.S.E.-listed company did: hire professionals to help out.

You've probably noticed that I've been stressing the problems that *individual* investors have with *individual* stocks. But don't get me wrong — that doesn't mean I don't like the stock market as an investment — far from it. Over time, if you employ professional management, you *are* often well rewarded through investing in the stock market, especially since the average return from stocks has historically been higher than the return from "safe" investments like interest-bearing bonds.

For those of you who meet their minimum investment requirements and where that minimum is an appropriate percentage of your asset base, a professional money manager called an *investment* counselor can help. These counselors are investment advisors registered with the SEC, and they manage *only* stock and bond portfolios, usually on a discretionary basis. Their minimum asset requirement is usually $250,000, but some investment counselors will consider a lesser amount as long as a minimum fee is met.

The professional money manager's full-time job is to study the market and select those companies whose shares they believe will perform to meet your goals. The counselor is motivated toward good performance because the more money you make, the more money he or she makes, for the fee charged by all money managers I'm aware of is a fixed percentage based on the value of your portfolio. The percentage will depend on the amount of money being managed, but typically ranges between ½ percent to 2 percent per year. If the money under management grows, the counselor's income increases, and vice versa. It's too bad that the SEC doesn't allow other professional advisors to also charge fees based on a performance basis.

Generally, investment counselors will (or should) inquire about your financial goals. You could want aggressive growth, or mostly income with some growth, something in between, or something else. Counselors will construct a portfolio for you based on the securities they follow, but they will never actually hold your assets: securities are usually held in your name at a bank or brokerage firm. Investment counselors do not receive commissions — in fact, they will often save you money on commissions because one of their functions is to direct transactions to brokerage firms that charge the least amount. If, however, you specify that you wish a particular person or firm to execute your trades, of course, the counselor will oblige you.

I'm sure it will come as no surprise to you when I say all investment counselors are not terrific. Just because a counselor spends all of his or her time selecting and monitoring stocks and bonds doesn't mean those investments will perform any better than if you had picked them yourself. Furthermore, it's not easy to measure a counselor's overall past performance: though managers will provide you with representative information about their accounts' performance, the portfolios they will show you are not, and cannot be, the exact portfolio you might desire. Also, the performance demonstrated will necessarily be from a different point in time, and the performance record will only include clients who have remained with the money manager, not those who left unhappy or dissatisfied.

Still, representative portfolio performance does provide some insight, and I continue to believe that most professional counselors will usually perform better than the investor would him or herself. It simply comes down to a matter of selecting the right counselor. In chapter 14, I'll provide you with my "sure-fire" method for selecting good investment counselors, as well as financial planners, lawyers, doctors, and some 20 other professionals as classified by law.

Incidentally, my system for finding a good money manager has yet to turn up a bank trust department. One of the reasons, I suspect, is that bank portfolio managers are paid like bankers, i.e., not very well. The better ones leave to establish their own firms, join independent firms, or become portfolio managers with mutual funds.

Another reason I'm against purchasing individual stocks is because of the availability of professional management through *mutual funds*.

Mutual funds are open-end investment companies (they continually create new shares on demand) that pool investors' money to obtain diversification and professional management. The pooling of capital allows you to enjoy diversification for as little as $100, something you could not achieve on your own or through investment counselors: your risk can be spread over a portfolio that may contain 100 or more holdings. And since the fund is managed by experienced, very well paid professionals, you don't need to bother researching and following individual stocks, or worry about what to buy and sell and when. In other words, you don't have to become an investment expert yourself.

Mutual funds can usually offer an abundance of services that are difficult to match elsewhere: check-writing privileges, periodic payments made to you monthly, quarterly, or in any time frame you desire, switching within the "family" of funds to a different fund if your objective changes (because different kinds of funds under common management serve different purposes), and more. They are also a very liquid investment, since the fund is obliged to redeem your shares on request. Additionally, a mutual fund's track record is a matter of public record, and, in general, over a period of time a fund will usually outperform an individual stock investor's track record.

Mutual funds may or may not charge a commission. If there is a standard broker charge (8 to 8 $1/2$ percent), it's called a "load" fund: if there is a half charge (typically 2 to 4 percent), it's called a "low-load" fund and if there is no charge, a "no-load" fund. You should not choose among funds merely on the basis of loads and fees — or, for that matter, any particular investment. A load fund that consistently produces a result that fits in well with your other investments might well be worth the extra cost. On the other hand, if a no-load fund produces similar results, your choice is obvious.

No-load mutual fund shares can be purchased only from the fund itself. Since there is no commission, you either have to do your own research to find a good fund, or seek a financial planner who has already researched and will recommend no-load mutual funds. Load and low-load fund shares can be purchased from a stockbroker or through most financial planners. This, of course, will provide you with someone to consult and talk with. In all cases, however, you will be handed or sent a fund prospectus. The law requires that this document, which tells you more about the fund than you ever wanted to know, must be in your hands before you can purchase any shares.

Mutual funds come in many shapes and sizes. You can go with funds that emphasize income, or safety, or growth, or tax-protection, or some combination of the above. You can go with funds that specialize in certain instruments — bond funds, for example, or even more specialized funds that invest only in federal government, municipal, corporate, or convertible bonds. You can find hybrid funds that are still more specific, serving just about every taste — aerospace and defense funds, emergency funds, financial services funds, gold funds, health care funds, leisure and entertainment funds, natural resources funds, or utility funds. And this list is by no means complete. The most common kind of mutual fund, however, is the least specialized — the money market fund, which we discussed in chapter 8.

Your first task is to sort through the various options and choose the type of fund that best fits your personal financial philosophy and goals: growth, income, tax savings, and so on. And I would not recommend that most of you get caught up in all the specialty funds. You want to keep it simple ... remember?

Generally, depending on your goals and investment comfort level, you'll want a standard "growth fund," as opposed to an "aggressive" growth fund. Middle-of-the-road growth funds invest in large, household-name companies such as General Electric, and aggressive growth funds do not; they invest in younger, more risk-prone companies. For the same reasons — safety and security — you'll probably want a high-quality bond fund, not a low-rated discount bond fund.

Your gains or losses in mutual fund investing will ultimately depend on how much you paid for them. Cheaper is better, of course, but since you can't really predict the best time to invest, I recommend you buy fund shares in fixed-dollar amounts on a regular basis rather than by lump sums that could hit the market just when share prices are at or near a peak. You might "dollar-cost-average" a $10,000 investment by investing $1,000 a month for 10 months. Dollar-cost-averaging saves you money because investing a fixed amount regularly ensures that you will buy fewer high-priced shares and more low-priced shares, since in the long term, the stock market does go up.

Since there are more than 800 funds in the marketplace today, an excellent place to begin your research is with a review of mutual fund performance records. You'll find such reviews in the August issue of *Forbes* and also in *Money* and *Business Week* magazines. Most local public libraries will have a reference copy of the "Wiesenburger Investment Companies Service" as well as other services, which lists the name, address, and investment philosophy of every mutual fund. If you hunger for still more information, the trade group called the Investment Company Institute (1775 K Street, N.W., Washington, D.C., 20005) publishes useful material on mutual funds, including a $2 Mutual Fund Fact Book. The No-Load Mutual Fund Association (11 Penn Plaza, No. 2204, New York, NY, 10117) will send you a free list of publications from which you can buy its own $2 Guide to Mutual Funds. Not bad — $4.44 budgeted for research, plus overhead, unless you use postcards.

Another professionally managed equity investment to consider is a *closed-end fund.* A closed-end fund has a fixed number of shares outstanding that are traded on the open market. The share price fluctuates according to supply and demand. Because an open-end mutual fund continually creates new shares to meet investor demand, the share price does not fluctuate. Both kinds of funds buy and sell securities in tune with their prospectus and with professional management's view of the marketplace and both have very diversified holdings. But many people don't like closed-end funds because the market value of their shares may bear no relationship to the value of the fund's holdings. Most closed-end funds sell at a 5 to 20 percent discount due to the idiosyncracies of the stock market, whereas the share value of the open-end fund always reflects the underlying holdings. Few of you will bother with closed-end funds anyway because the choice of funds is so limited.

Let me emphasize once again that the kind of fund you choose will depend on what you seek. Many people choose money market funds because they act like flexible savings accounts, but that doesn't mean such a fund is right for you. If you don't need income from the money targeted for this investment, for example, you probably don't want a fixed-dollar mutual fund — you might be better off with a variable-dollar growth fund. Then again, if it's your first investment, you may want more safety and thus should avoid the possible volatility of a growth fund.

If, however, you choose a fund you later become unhappy with, re-member that it's usually very easy to switch from one mutual fund to another. Furthermore, as your goals and circumstances change, you can readily redirect your money to new ends.

Chapter 11

"EASY" MONEY

Money is a strange animal. If you have $1 million in assets, you won't feel wealthy. If you have $10,000 in cash, you will because that's a LOT of cash. Similarly, if you make money too quickly, you tend not to take it seriously. You cannot relate to an instant $100,000 profit when ordinarily it takes you one, two, three, four, or more years to earn that kind of money. It becomes "monopoly" or "poker-chip money" — not real.

Most people are financially conservative. Though you wouldn't turn down easy money, you already know that high rewards require high risk. And most of you should not get involved in high-risk money situations because you cannot afford the potential high loss. Yet my description of the money-go-round would not be complete if I didn't inform you about some of the more common paths to "easy" money. Someday I hope you will have all your basic financial needs covered. For only then, if you wish, could some of you "step out" with some of your money and join those who always hear a different financial drummer. Their beat is brassy, exciting, and usually out of tune; but sometimes it's just right, and then their beat really can't be beat. These people are the great speculators, the "life in the fast lane" people.

This type of speculator will get involved in commodities, long-shot stocks, really junk bonds, currencies, very high risk venture capital, and more — you name it, they'll invest in it. They are always hoping for overnight success by trading on inside rumors, putting all their money on one chip (often silicon), betting on the weather forecast or the direction of skirt hemlines. When a deal begins to go sour, which is frequently, they often compound their difficulties by adding more money to the pot instead of cutting their losses. Often, pockets empty, they have to give up. At that point some of them learn a valuable lesson: the difference between genuine *investing* and (different degrees of) *speculation*.

Speculation is not for the cautious, and it's hardly conducive to "money ease." But that doesn't mean you can't ever buy frozen orange juice futures — far from it. What it means is that if you ever do become interested in speculation, you should do enough research to turn highly speculative deals into those more approaching investment quality. Remember, in this field you'll go broke trying to outguess the experts. You either have to become an expert yourself or find a way to use the experts' knowledge. Your investments will still be rather risky, but at least you won't be throwing your money away. And there's always a chance, if you've played your cards right, to hit the jackpot.

The cardinal rule of risky investing is putting up only what you can afford to lose. That requirement alone eliminates many potential investors. Those who can, however, might be in for some real excitement, for venture capital is indeed play money — "extra" money, cash you can say goodbye to without breaking down in tears. But spare cash isn't the only thing you need; you also need to have a strong will and, well, courage. This kind of investing is not for everyone; it's usually for those who thrive on excitement and tension, who like the challenge of trying to turn small opportunities into big gains.

FOREIGN MONEY

Investing in foreign currency isn't always a highly speculative investment. In fact, many people buy it as a hedge. If the U.S. dollar goes down, your assets in other currencies may correspondingly increase in value. But is is also true that pure money instruments can be volatile, even more so than gold or oil. In the 1920s, at one time it took *3 million* German marks to buy a single dollar. If we enter a time of crisis, some currencies may indeed prove as valuable as gold, but it is hard to say which ones.

If you decide to attempt speculative investing, foreign currency is probably a good place to start. For one thing, investing is easy, and you can begin with a very small amount of money. You can buy most investment-quality currencies through a foreign exchange broker, or certain brokerage firms, for about a 3 percent markup. You'll also be able to sell your investment quickly if you have to, with no penalty for haste. Best of all, however, you can see how your investment is doing every day, just by reading your newspaper's business pages and tracking currency exchange rates against the dollar. You'll soon notice, too, how the news affects exchange rates, and that may give you a fair idea of where the currencies you hold are going.

In recent years, the soundest foreign currencies to invest in have been the West German mark, the Swiss franc, and the Japanese yen. Somewhat riskier investments would be other European currencies; riskier yet would be just about anything else. As with most investments, timing is everything; when the U.S. dollar is near historic highs, as was true in 1984, it's only a matter of time before the dollar weakens and other currencies grow stronger. Still, the dollar could turn around and hit even higher highs.

You can also hold foreign currency investments that produce income. There is an active market in foreign bonds, which pay interest and can be bought through a number of U.S. brokerage firms. You can also buy a foreign currency future contract and foreign currency endowments and annuities. And as I mentioned earlier, you can also buy stock in foreign companies, which is, of course, a less direct way of investing in foreign money.

JUNK BONDS

Junk bonds are those in which the bond graders — Standard and Poor's, Moody's, and other companies — have serious doubts about whether the issuer has the ability to pay the interest or principal when due. On a scale in which the highest rating is AAA, junk bonds are rated BB or lower, which means there is a greater risk if you buy them. Consequently, they sell at great discounts — often more than 50 percent off face value. If the issuing company returns to financial health, you've got a winner. But if it doesn't, you'll take a beating if you wish to sell ... that is, if the company is still in business.

Junk bonds, almost by definition, are not safe. And numbers don't always tell the full story. From 1900 to 1945, junk bonds did yield 50 percent more interest income than higher quality issues, and from 1945 to 1984 their yields were on average more than 4 percent higher than those of high-grade bonds. But these are merely averages. True, defaults are rare — less than 0.2 percent of the bonds available in the past 40 years — but a very large number of individual bonds did not perform well when compared to other investments. Thus, because it lessens the risk of individual bonds defaulting, the deversification offered by a mutual fund portfolio of junk bonds makes more sense than purchasing them individually.

PENNY STOCKS

Penny stocks, properly diversified, are perhaps the best "crap shoot" for your spare money. Stocks that trade from less than 5 cents a share to $3 a share offer you the opportunity to buy a lot of stock, and a wide variety of stocks, with your "mad money." Not only will you feel good about owning so many shares (you really feel you have a "position" in a company!), but you will possibly double or triple your money within two or three years, if just one of those stocks takes off.

A young client of mine once purchased $2,500 worth of a very low-priced oil stock traded on the Denver exchange (as are many penny stocks). The company hit, and, of course, so did he. Within six months the value of his stock had jumped to $13,000. Ironically, but typically, it was the worst thing that could have happened to him. He was a first-time buyer and quickly reinvested. He learned just as quickly that his magic touch was nothing but luck, for his very nice profit was soon gone.

FUTURES

Penny stocks sound quite inviting; anyone can afford to lose pennies. But when I say *commodities* or *futures contracts,* most people become frightened, for here real dollars are involved. Some 300,000 people trade commodity futures every year, and as with individual stocks, only even more so, the vast majority of them lose money. Commodities, however, are much more dangerous, for you can also lose *more* money than you started out with.

The odds are against you to begin with, and sink even lower when you consider your fellow traders. Many of them are full-timers who do nothing but trade commodities: they win the futures game more than most other people. They succeed, in large part, by outfoxing inexperienced traders, which is most of us. In order to play the game, the commodities investor must know a lot about what he or she is trading and do so at the right time. It's difficult to predict the future, of course, but if you happen to have some expertise with some kind of investments, you may be able to turn commodities trading into something more than a blind gamble.

The secret, and danger, of trading futures is *leverage.* When you buy a futures contract — whether for traditional commodities like pork bellies or for other investments like silver — all you need part with is 10 percent of the purchase price. Many investors are attracted to futures because of that low deposit or "margin" needed to buy a contract. With little of his or her money involved, the investor stands to make a lot of other people's money, or if things don't work out, lose his or her shirt, shoes, and socks because this leverage places you at personal risk, whereas real estate leverage does not.

When you buy a contract, you agree to buy something at a given price at a future date; you're betting that the price will go up, so you can sell your investment later, at a profit. When you sell a contract, you're betting on the opposite — that the sale price you agree to today is higher than the market price of your investment at the specified sale date. The typical contract lasts only three weeks, and the buyer rarely takes delivery, so you don't have to worry about having thousands of pounds of pork bellies delivered to your home. Although they were created as a business hedge and are still effectively used for that purpose, commodities are mostly regarded as a quick means to make or lose money.

Aside from understanding the nature of the investments you want to trade, there is little you can do to gain an edge over other traders. Commodities trading, in fact, is as much art as science; temperament and intuition are probably as important as timing and knowledge. For that reason, beginning traders should trade on paper for a time, keeping track of gains and loses, before entering the market. (This advice also applies, of course, to almost every speculative investment.) If you are successful in the safety of your home or office, you may have what it takes. The real futures market is far more challenging, however, so if and when you play for keeps, you should start out using less leverage and perhaps only one-eighth of your earmarked commodities capital to keep your losses (and gains) small.

If you make a plan and stick to it, you may be able to become one of the few traders who profit in the futures market. Those who do follow a few simple rules of thumb.

Create stop points for all your purchases, so if prices fall to that level, you'll sell the contract and take the small loss. Trade only when you have the right opportunity, not just when you have some extra cash. Be wary of commission costs, don't trade on every rumor, and keep your wits about you. And remember that successful traders can distinguish trending markets from trading markets, moving at once when they've spotted a sure trend.

Above all else, don't take a position you can't handle. A dramatic adverse price movement can be ruinous and can turn an exciting investment into a disaster. You would do well to consider creating a commodities pool completely separate from your other investments and also consider professional management or advice, because commodities are likely to be by far the most speculative and dangerous element in your portfolio.

VENTURE INVESTING

If you had invested seed money (no pun intended) in Apple Computer some 10 years ago, at one point you would have had a profit of approximately 50,000 percent. One investor I know actually achieved a staggering 177,000 percent profit through venture capital investing. Just *think* of all the "spare" money he now has! But how many people invest in the right companies at the right time? And how many of those were doing more than guesswork, and how many got out with *any* profit? The answer is, very few: most people who become wealthy through investing in start-up companies have been, in a word, lucky. Nonetheless, venture capital investing can be a valid sort of investment if you have a well-balanced portfolio. Today, venture capital investments have achieved enough respectability that pension funds, insurance companies, and banks are large investors. The state of Michigan is now the nation's second largest venture funder, setting aside over $650 million of its Employees Retirement Pension Fund for venture capital.

There are always thousands of new companies around seeking venture capital, and most of them are going to fail. High technology —

the largest area for this type of investment — has many winners, but keep in mind that the *average* annual investment return, over the past twenty years, has been just 22 percent (30 to 35 percent for the past 10 years). While the overall numbers are indeed excellent, if you remove some of the superwinners, the average annual return would not equal passbook savings interest. As a prospective venture investor, you want to avoid these failed business that bring the return rate down and find the likely winners — not just those with potential.

No matter which company you invest in, the odds will still be long — that is, after all, what venture capital investment is all about. In order to reduce your risk you need to investigate the field, separate the prospects from the phantoms, and sometimes target a return rate of as much as 100 to one if you are considering funding raw start-up operations with "seed money." Here you'll be joining the initial investor's family, friends, and doctor by putting money into Albert's new idea.

A less risky venture capital investment is at the next funding period, at the second round, or intermediate stage, before a company has matured sufficiently to consider an initial public offering. The third round, or mezzanine level, is when the company is about to go public. However, regardless of the investment state you choose, there must be intensive investigation. And investigation means research — research usually far beyond the capabilities of most investors. Good research is not reading about a company in the morning paper, or a tip from a friend of a friend. You can count on the fact that 99 $\frac{1}{2}$ times out of 100, by that time you'll already be at the end of the investment dog pack. What you are likely to need is professional management of your venture money or, at the very least, good professional advice. Professional venture capitalists have a good working knowledge of the area, a full-time commitment to the business, and know how to diversify. That full-time involvement, such as sitting on the board, is necessary because professional venture capitalists can add value to an investee company and increase its chances for success. Such involvement can also include assistance in hiring personnel, financial guidance, and the benefit of having "been there before."

Diversification is to venture capital what location is to real estate. Losses are expected, but the gains on successful companies can greatly exceed those losses. When selecting an early-stage investment, for example, a good venture capitalist requires a reasonable probability of a return on the investment of 10 to 15 times within five years. If dollars were then invested equally in ten companies and only one achieves its expected return, investors would still have their capital returned — despite the complete failure of the others.

And knowledge comes from exposure and experience. Venture capitalists review hundreds of business plans, which provides them with an awareness of markets and competitive developments that nonprofessional investors rarely have.

There are several methods through which you can gain professional management and still choose the level of risk you wish to take. Registered limited partnerships are available that lower risk by investing in a number of ventures and greatly expand investor participation in high technology. And at affordable prices, too — you can invest in some public partnerships for as little as $5,000. But a private placement minimum investment often starts at $100,000.

You can also invest in high technology through specialized venture-oriented mutual funds that invest mostly in companies that are already public. That means, of course, you won't be getting in on the ground floor. Some have done well, doubling or tripling their share value while the stocks were hot, but now most reflect the general decline in high-tech issues and are off more than 50 percent from their highs.

Individual stocks are another way to invest in high-tech companies. But as with specialized mutual funds, with this investment you've missed out on the greatest chance to participate in the company's growth *before* it went public. And if you invest in just one company, you have no diversity. Since making money in this area is so difficult, you'd be taking a high risk for what would probably be an unspectacular return, and that's not the best way to go about investing your venture capital. Even in this area — perhaps especially here — you should make your money work as intelligently as you can.

There are still other ways to invest a relatively small number of dollars in high-tech companies while acquiring a diversified portfolio. There are closed-end funds that are required by law to invest most of your money in the shares of companies that are already public. And there are also SBICs (small-business investment corporations) and

BDCs (business development corporations). They can invest large amounts of money in companies that have not yet gone public.

Now that you are "fully" educated, I recommend you seek venture capital investments that have potentially unlimited upside potential and that you consider the limited partnership as your primary investment vehicle. Make sure, however, that the general partners are independent and not promoting or developing the new venture as well: conflicts of interest do occur. If possible you should also select a program that will invest in a variety of ventures. There are numerous single-venture programs — sort of like a one-well oil deal — and these are very, very risky.

You should also seek a general partner with the necessary skills to structure the partnership most favorably for tax purposes. Venture capital investments and research and development can frequently be structured to obtain tax deductions as well as growth income. They can sometimes provide a 30- to 80-percent tax deduction in the year of investment. I don't view these projects as tax shelters, however, as most of the venture-capital limited partnerships have deductions at the lower end of the scale.

In conclusion, it is easy to get caught up in the glamour and excitement of venture capital investing, particularly in the high-tech industry. If the automobile industry had moved as quickly as high tech, today we would be able to buy a Rolls Royce for under $10 and get 500 miles to a gallon of gas. But high technology, despite all the hype and hoopla, is subject to the same economic trends and business principles as more mundane industries. That's why the quality and competence of the general partner — your business partner — is especially important.

The general partner is the one who places the "value added" into a partnership, no matter which kind of partnership you're in. He or she always has the difficult task of determining the difference between hype and ripe. And you always have the difficult task of selecting the better general partners, which you'll be able to do with the help of my guidelines in this book's final chapter.

• PART V •

Guarding Your Assets

• Chapter 12

SAFETY FROM THE STORM

In 1929 most Americans never thought the stock market could crash. Many stockholders were completely wiped out; hundreds of thousands of citizens lost their jobs. We're told that such a crash can never recur, and that may well be true, but then again, inflation was not supposed to hit double digits either. Was the energy crisis only a figment of our imagination? Is the federal budget balanced? Do we import as many goods as we export, thus achieving a balance of trade? No, no, and no. These are three of the many good reasons to prepare for possible stormy economic times.

PRECIOUS METALS

Precious metals like gold, silver, and platinum are a prudent hedge against bad times brought about by political upheaval, international economic turmoil, inflation, and the like. As I mentioned earlier, for example, they can hedge against inflationary pressures that usually devalue the worth of fixed savings. Frequently the very same factors that cause many investments to erode in value cause precious metals to increase dramatically in price. A precious metals position can thus be viewed as a portfolio hedge as well as a reasonable investment in itself.

Investing in precious metals in general, and gold in particular, has been viewed, at least in this country, as a highly speculative endeavor. And there is a reason for that perception: gold's short-term price volatility has been quite pronounced since 1971, when it became a freely floated commodity (no longer restricted to a $35 an ounce price). More recently, however, most investment advisors have become aware of gold's usefulness as an investment vehicle, principally because of its ability to maintain purchasing power.

Gold is volatile, certainly, but there still exists a 4,000-year historical uptrend for this precious metal. As a result, I recommend that you consider purchasing gold as a hedge or as an investment on a very long-term basis, not as a trading vehicle. You should hold on to your core position through good *and* bad markets, for even the metals experts have a lot of difficulty deciding when to get in and when to get out.

I generally recommend that precious metals take up from 3 to 10 percent of the value of a diversified portfolio. As with growth mutual funds, you should accumulate your position over time in order to "dollar-cost-average" — a particularly important purchasing method when you're dealing with a volatile investment. I recommend a disciplined plan, such as investing monthly, quarterly, semiannually, before each marriage, birth, divorce, grandchild . . . name your pleasure. Another recommendation: if the price of metals changes so much that it unbalances the value of the rest of your portfolio, you should add or reduce your position, as the case may be, to bring the percentages back into line.

Your investment can consist of actual metal through coins or bullion; certificates representing ownership of metals stored in the U.S. or abroad; individual mining stocks; or a mutual fund that invests in diversified mining stocks. The advantage of mining stocks is that they pay dividends, and that can provide some protection against the price volatility of metals investment. The disadvantage of mining stocks (and certificates of ownership, for that matter) is that they represent ownership of metals-related assets, not the tangible metals themselves. If you actually own metals, you are investing *directly* in metal, and that may be a significant advantage in an emergency, when gold or silver coins are likely to be more useful to you than paper. But it's also true that in a dire emergency, coins may well be less marketable than food or ammunition anyway.

You should also take into consideration the fact that most of the world's gold comes from South Africa and that their mining stocks (and thus mutual funds investing in these stocks) bear political, thus economic, risks that are not present in U.S. or Canadian mining stocks. Furthermore, many of you may have political sensitivity with regard to South Africa. If you do not, then the fact that South African stocks pay much higher dividends may partly offset the political risk disadvantage.

From among the various choices, I recommend you invest in precious metals through a mutual fund that buys mining stocks. A fund has several advantages over other metals investment vehicles. First, the fund is composed of a diversified group of metals stocks that pay dividends; metal coins, bullion, and certificates, by contrast, pay no current income, and bullion usually carries storage, assay, and insurance costs. Second, the fund is liquid and can be converted to cash easily. Third, you are gaining professional management that not only closely monitors the political situation and the stocks, but also physically visits the mines. Fourth, you can start or add to your mutual fund metal portfolio anytime and for as little as $5; metal coins and bullion purchases, however, must be in greater dollar amounts.

Now that I've said that, let me put this metal business in perspective. If you're like most people, you probably have a difficult time thinking of gold as a hedge and purchasing it for that reason. A precious metal investment is usually at the bottom of your priority list, and will remain there unless you get caught up in "gold fever" or think it's a good speculation. I really believe that you should purchase *some* precious metals, and your financial advisors can further discuss how. But if you can't get motivated to do so, the world won't collapse. However, if you don't and it does, you will be sorry you didn't . . . or something like that.

GEMS

Like precious metals and other noncurrency securities, gemstones can also hedge your other investments. But hedging with gems — blue sapphires, emeralds, rubies, diamonds, and the like — is not something I generally recommend, for a number of reasons. There is no central exchange that records gemstone prices; there is no well-standardized grading system and no adequate pricing system. In short, there is little reason to hedge your portofolio through gems unless you wish to wait five years just to break even.

I am aware that some people have fled burning houses and political revolutions with their entire net worth, sometimes a fortune, in their pockets. They have done it with gemstones, usually diamonds. But if you're like most of us, you're probably better off buying gems for their beauty.

COLLECTIBLES

Runaway inflation — and the fear of it — kept the collectible market hot for years. The market is not so hot today; however, collectibles, like precious metals, can still be an excellent investment — with the emphasis on the "can."

The dictionary defines a collectible as something that is gathered for a hobby. Most collectibles can offer this personal pleasure since they are tangible and you can keep them near you to look at and enjoy.

Almost anything can be considered a collectible. What all have in common is that no collectible generates income and each is appreciated by the collector because of perceived beauty or intrinsic rarity. Due to this rarity, certain collectibles have even achieved investment caliber status and their ownership has become a status symbol. Typical collectibles of investment caliber are antiques, artwork, classic cars, coins, stamps, Chinese ceramics, oriental rugs, and photographs. Collectibles that usually fall into the hobby category are Shirley Temple dolls, fountain pens, comic books, campaign buttons, autographs, baseball cards, shells, mugs, telephones, doorknobs, and matchbooks, to name just a few. The hobby and investment categories may overlap, sometimes with excellent results: one collector came to my office recently soon after he had sold *part* of his baseball card collection for $200,000. Despite the sale, he says, he still has one of the largest such collections in the world.

His experience, of course, is highly unusual. Most of the time there is a real risk in collectibles, primarily because collectors have to be extremely knowledgeable about their chosen field. Most of us don't have the time to gain that knowledge, and so can't make the "right" purchases. Sizable commissions and fees are often involved, too, which means that your profit may be quickily eaten up by buying and selling costs. Lastly, even investment collectibles often tend to become personal assets rather than financial assets. Many people buy paintings as investments — or at least say they do — and then can't bear to part with them. If it has appreciated in the meantime, the art has become an appreciated personal asset like a home and shouldn't be looked at as part of the financial portfolio.

Numismatic Investments

Among the more popular collectibles are coins and currency, which probably also have the broadest market. The supply of any given coin or currency note is limited to the total number struck or printed during a particular year at a specific mint. Mintage figures are published, verifiable, and precise (quite a contrast to the numbers bandied about in the gem market). These figures only give us a yardstick for measuring the actual, current supply of coins and currency, however, for it constantly diminishes over time. Many experts believe that 95 to 99 percent of all original rare coins have been lost, destroyed, or melted down to metal once again.

When you look into purchasing a numismatic investment, or any collectible, it is important to buy the best you can afford and to think in terms of a long-term commitment due to the markup. And you should consider diversifying your collectibles investment — for example, buying not only gold but copper, nickel, and silver coins, as well as coins from different years, mints, and nations.

Coins and currencies performed well in 1984 despite low inflation, appreciating more than 20 percent according to *Fact* magazine. But don't let that isolated figure deceive you: the same magazine shows that if you had purchased the coins *three years before,* your increase was still only 22 percent. Which means a $10,000 coin purchased at the beginning of 1984 would have been worth $12,000 at the year's end. But a $10,000 purchase three years before would have only appreciated to a $12,200 value. To make sure that such performance figures do not mislead you, it's imperative that you work with a well-established, reputable dealer and together study performance figures over various periods of time.

Philatelic Investments

Stamp collecting is another hobby that can take a lot of money, though it doesn't have to. Like so many other collectibles, stamps don't require a large initial investment; after all, you probably started collecting as a child, using your allowance money. Stamps, like coins, should be held for many years. I still have a numbered block of stamps I purchased more than 30 years ago for $3.60. A genuine expert told me at the time, "Hold on to them, kid, they'll make you rich some day," and I'm still holding. Last time I checked, about two years ago, my block was worth $36. Fortunately, I'm the patient sort.

If you're serious (or optimistic) about investing in stamps, it may be worthwhile to hire a knowledgeable advisor or agent to make acquisitions for you. These advisors charge a 5 to 10 percent commission for each purchase.

Art

Art is one of the most popular collectibles. For convenience, I'm going to concentrate on paintings and prints, but the criteria I set below also apply to books, antiques, jewelry, silver, and other display-for-pleasure items.

Purchasing art is not like buying stock; you don't phone your broker and ask to buy 100 old prints. So whatever you do, get expert help. Deal only with reputable galleries and dealers who know the business — where, what, and when to buy and sell. Never compromise on quality. Buy works of established artists. Don't speculate until you're knowledgeable about art values and understand the risks. And remember, you are buying for your own esthetic appreciation as well as capital appreciation, so wait for what you want. If your purchase appreciates significantly in value, consider that a bonus.

By the way, be sure to consider insuring your more valuable collectibles and have them formally appraised every year. That kind of information is almost essential if your collectibles are stolen or damaged. At the very least, take pictures of your valuables: a description, no matter how detailed, hardly takes the place of a photograph. A picture of a picture is worth two thousand words.

I say "consider" insuring your collectibles because many people may not want to replace a lost or stolen art object. If that's the case, there is little reason to pay high insurance premiums.

NATURAL RESOURCES

A hedge-oriented investment in natural resources can be a double-edged sword. Because natural resources are finite investments, they will theoretically become more valuable as they are consumed. Land in or near urban areas, for example, has appreciated tremendously over the past two decades because you can't create new, centrally located parcels. On the other hand, some resources do in fact run out (or can't be resold), and so have a limited lifetime. Oil and gas wells won't pump forever, for example, and their returns will eventually cease.

The curious contradiction in natural resources is the fact that the *demand* for them almost always increases. In that sense, oil and land are unlike gold or diamonds, which can also be considered natural resources; gold and diamonds are valued for their traditional worth, while oil and land are (usually) valued for their actual worth. Without natural resources, this country grinds to a halt, as we saw during the Arab oil boycott of the 1970s.

Although some people regard these kinds of investments as highly speculative, the best ones are not. We've all heard about Florida swampland and oil drilling lottery scams, and there are a number of charlatans in this area. But if you investigate thoroughly, you'll find a number of investments that are just about as safe as anything else in your portfolio. They are intended not only to hedge your dollars, but also to provide growth, and many of them can also provide significant income.

Energy investments have been popular ever since the oil crisis, for a good reason. Many of the highly touted alternative energy investments, however, have not proved to be good investments; nuclear power is currently in disfavor, solar power has yet to live up to its potential, the development of wind and geothermal energy sources is still experimental and done only on a very small scale. Some of the investments in these areas have provided major tax write-offs, but a good investment should give you more than that. Thus, the one energy investment that I consistently recommend is the old standby — oil.

Oil investments can be made through purchases of individual stocks, mutual funds, leases, futures, oil and gas programs in production, and drilling. I prefer an investment in an oil and gas income fund, because these are public partnerships offering direct investments in a diversified portfolio of already producing oil and gas wells. The partnerships pool your funds with those of other investors and purchase interests in a large number of existing oil and gas properties that are geologically and geographically diversified. Production from each well is then sold; the income flows back to the partnership and is distributed to the investor on a quarterly basis. The partnership program is somewhat analogous to a mutual fund investing in producing oil and gas properties.

Oil and gas income programs offer many advantages over more traditional income vehicles. You are purchasing established resources, so there is no drilling involved, which is where much of the risk of oil investing lies. The investment traditionally has produced a tax-favored income comparable to, and often higher than, the income provided by long-term corporate bonds.

If you believe, as I do, that existing energy resources will always be in demand — particularly oil for *at least* the next 10 years — you should seriously consider an oil income fund as both a hedge and an investment: as a portfolio hedge, because oil prices, during an inflationary time, have been at the forefront of the price rise; and as an investment, because oil provides an excellent, mostly sheltered, high rate of income that also has some liquidity — once a year the general partners usually offer to repurchase the investor's interest. Now is a good time to buy, too, because oil prices are down. As Bernard Baruch once said about timing one's purchases, "Buy straw hats in the fall."

Oil and gas income programs can also be used to fund life insurance trusts, short-term reversionary (Clifford) trusts, pension profit-sharing plans, IRAs, and Keogh plans. You can learn more about them from investment advisors and financial planners, as well as most brokerage firms.

INTERNATIONAL MUTUAL FUNDS

International mutual funds are an important hedge as well. Diversification of your growth portfolio with global and international mutual funds can be very useful because national stock markets often fluctuate independently of one another. The U.S. stock market, for example, may be declining at the same time the Japanese market is posting advances. By dividing your holdings into securities of both countries, you reduce the overall volatility of your portfolio and lower your risk. I typically recommend that clients place 25 to 35 percent of the money they have earmarked for a stock market investment into international mutual funds.

A foreign stock investment can provide an additional benefit. When the value of the other country's currency rises in relation to the dollar, so does the value of those stockholdings. The reverse, of course, is also true.

Though regarded with suspicion by most American investors, these funds have performed better over the years than most domestic funds. The U.S. market's share, in dollars, of the world's 18 major equity markets declined to 50 percent in 1980, down from 70 percent over the previous 15 years. And between 1970 and 1980, it ranked only 15th in total return. If your portfolio doesn't include an interest in foreign securities, you're missing not only half the investment possibilities in world stock markets, but a very favorable investment opportunity in general.

You have a choice of 17 international funds, which invest chiefly in foreign securities, or 21 global funds, which invest in both foreign and U.S. stocks. The minimum investment is typically $1,000. Again, you can learn more about these funds (both load and no-load) from a broker, investment advisor, or financial planner.

Chapter 13

SAFETY FROM THE IRS

If you're like most people, you haven't quite finished the job of guarding your portfolio and income. There remains a financial trap from which you may still be unprotected — the tax laws, as interpreted by the IRS. U.S. Supreme Court Justice Robert Jackson once said, "The United States has a system of taxation by confession," to which I add, "Confession is good for the soul but not the checkbook."

If you're unhappy about the amount of income tax you pay, you've got justification — taxation is growing faster than income. Since we started paying taxes, the annual income taxes paid by the average family have increased *32 times* faster than its income. All is not lost, however: Congress has provided many convenient techniques for minimizing tax liabilities, many of which I've mentioned in previous chapters. Tax-free municipal bonds; U.S. savings bonds; IRAs and Keoghs; deferred annuities; and various pension, profit-sharing, and deferred compensation plans are but a few of the ways you can reduce tax liability. Even IRA rollovers (the movement of the proceeds from a distributed qualified retirement plan to another investment without tax consequence) allow your currently unneeded money to grow and compound tax-deferred: you don't pay taxes on the income until you withdraw the money at retirement, when your tax bracket should be lower. Properly used, these investments can and do provide a great deal of tax sheltering. Unfortunately, most people don't take full advantage of them.

TAX REDUCTION PROCEDURES

I wonder sometimes what would happen to the financial planning profession if it weren't for taxes. Taxes are a great motivator. Tax filing is the only event I can think of (other than a shotgun wedding) in which deadlines are absolutely firm. Your choice . . . pay or die. Although the tax man's jolt is intended to put money in the government's coffers, it performs another useful purpose as well — reminding people of their personal financial planning or, more often, the lack of it.

I sometimes call paying taxes "bleeding," for that's how many people feel about it — that they are being bled to death by the IRS. With a quiver in his or her voice a new client will say, "I've got to do *something* to lower my tax bill." Or a client will say, "I've been paying my fair share of taxes all these years; I've paid enough. You've *got* to help me lower my taxes." Or as one particular client says, "I've bought my last MX missile."

I can't forget one desperate phone call I received from a person who said he was single, had recently moved into the higher tax brackets, and found that taxes were eating him alive. He complained so bitterly for 15 minutes, I assumed he was making well over $100,000. He was making $23,000 a year.

It's the "got to save taxes" syndrome. For some of you, it becomes such a big issue that you'll purchase the first (or every) tax shelter you hear about in order to avoid paying income taxes. That is not, of course, the logical order; it's the tax tail wagging the income dog. Before you even consider investing in a tax shelter, you should step back, re-examine your personal goals, and determine how tax avoidance fits into your plans.

An important thing to remember is that the best tax avoidance is achieved not through tax shelter, but through tax *procedures*. Why? Because the procedural solution always involves lower risk. As it is in medicine, where doctors consider the lowest-risk solutions, such as change in diet, before higher-risk approaches like surgery, so it should be with tax reduction: only after all procedural solutions have been exhausted should you turn to tax shelters.

What are these procedures? They are courses of action that don't involve investing. There are a lot of them, and I can't possibly cover them all, although I do cover many. For a more complete rundown you need to see your financial planner or tax advisor or continue to read the publications I've mentioned before: just about every procedure is written about eventually.

I have already mentioned IRAs and Keoghs. Though many people mistakenly assume these retirement plans are specific investments, in fact they are tax-saving procedures — shells that shelter an investment from taxes until your retirement.

Clifford trusts and outright gifts of income-producing assets are related procedures. They do not produce tax deductions; instead, they shift taxable income from a higher bracket to a lower bracket. Low- or no-interest loans can also accomplish this goal. When a family member loans money to another family member — often a child — in a lower tax bracket, the principal is taxed at the recipient's bracket.

Tax-saving procedures should be kept in mind throughout the year. Some years, of course, you'll find that it's already November or December before you've been able to look seriously at your tax situation. Ideally, that shouldn't happen, but I want to be realistic in this book, so I'll note there are still a few things you can do to lower your tax bill even very late in the year. By deferring income to the following year, or by taking advantage of the many available tax deductions, you can at least dull the tax bite. You must, of course, act before December 31, and should consider what effect your last-minute tax actions will have on current income and on any future tax legislation.

With the exception of an interest limitation, almost all forms of interest, as you probably know, are deductible from your federal income tax. That's one reason you might consider paying back loans late in the year and reborrowing the money early in the following year. This might not be such a good idea if your loan carries an early-repayment penalty or interest rates have gone up, but if interest rates have gone down, you'll be able to deduct your previous interest payments as well as enjoy lower future payments. If you anticipate having to pay additional state income taxes beyond salary withholding and estimated taxes, you may want to pay them early as well — unless altered by Congress, they too can be taken as itemized deductions on your federal taxes.

Certain purchases made this year can also reduce your tax bill. If you're planning to buy a car in the near future, remember that the state sales tax on automobiles (also boats, mobile homes, and motorcycles) is deductible, in addition to the standard sales tax deduction calculated according to income. You may also want to get medical or dental work done, or prepay for such expenses, or prepay medical insurance premiums. You may find it more economical to spend for medical help now than wait until January or February. You also may wish to pay your financial planner's bill (thank you) before the end of the year or those of other financial advisors, like your accountant.

When it comes to year-end income you don't need, you may find it makes sense to reverse this timing process — to delay receiving money until January. You can put off your billing until then or send bills out so late in December that you won't get paid until next year. Or you could buy a Treasury bill (as mentioned earlier) that doesn't pay interest until January, even though much of its earnings will accrue in the current year. In any case, consider carefully whether you might in fact need that money this year and whether you might not be overloading next year's income. Otherwise, you may just have the same problem again the following year — only worse.

Capital Gains and Losses

If you planned your taxes properly, by the end of the year your tax problems are already under control. You'll have deferred enough income to lower your tax bracket or created enough deductions to offset some income. But out of the blue a capital gain shows up — they are, after all, a primary goal of investing.

Capital gains are created by realizing, through sale, the appreciated gain in an asset, and they are taxed at a lower rate than income. If you've held the asset less than six months, you've got a *short-term* capital gain, which is fully taxed; if you've held the asset more than six months, as you probably should have, you've got *long-term* capital gain. Unless altered by Congress, only 40 percent of long-term gains need be reported to the IRS, and since currently the highest federal tax bracket is 50 percent, the effective federal tax rate for long-term capital gains is no higher than 20 percent. And there are proposals to even further reduce that rate.

Though they are not heavily taxed, these gains can be offset against capital losses. If you have, say, a $1,000 capital gain and you have an unrealized capital loss, you should try to establish at least a $1,000 of that capital loss. If the loss is smaller, you'll pay taxes on the difference; but if the loss is bigger, it's not wasted — the "excess" loss can be used to offset other income that same year, up to a maximum of $3,000. If the loss is short-term, it offsets your income dollar-for-dollar; if the loss is long-term, however, one dollar of loss offsets only 50 cents of income (note that short-term offsets are calculated first). If your capital losses, whether short-term or long-term are still not used up, they can be carried forward to offset, in the same way, capital gains and income in future years.

Confused? Well, don't worry — I'm not trying to turn you into a tax expert. I just want to make the point that you can establish capital losses or gains in order to offset gains or losses. Recently, a client who was "bleeding" to the tune of more than $100,000 a year learned this valuable tax-saving procedure. He had an investment counselor for his stock and bond portfolio (and had for many years), and he had an accountant . . . but no one told him he might be able to avoid high tax bills if he started taking capital losses. We did, and immediately reduced his tax bill by $80,000. If he really liked the stocks he sold, he could repurchase them after a short wait.

If you sell an asset for tax reasons, but your financial game plan calls for continued ownership of such an asset, you can sell the stock or bond, realize the loss, and then buy a security of a comparable company in the same industry. If you want to buy back the exact same security, however, or a similar one issued by the same company, you can't make the repurchase within 30 days of the selling date. The IRS considers a shorter waiting period to be a "wash sale" of assets and will disallow the offset. If you're afraid the market will rise during this waiting period, you could "double up" on your loss shares — buy the same number of shares you already own, wait the 31 days, and then sell the half of the stock with the higher cost basis.

Losses are particularly easy to establish with municipal bonds. If you want to increase your municipal bond yield, consolidate your holdings, or just establish a new maturity date, you can sell the bonds at a loss and replace them with the desired bonds whether issued by the same municipality or not. Such bond "swaps" are not considered wash sales by the IRS.

Bonds issued by different corporations can also be "swapped" and avoid the 30-day rule. This is more difficult with corporate assets than with tax-free bonds, however, because fewer maturity dates are available from the private sector. If you have money in a mutual fund, you'll find you can establish a short-term capital loss by switching from one mutual fund to another within the same family of funds. The IRS considers each switch within a fund family to be a sale and new purchase. If you have just purchased a load fund, you can take a loss — usually the amount of your broker's commission — and later repurchase the fund desired in the first place, often for only a $5 fee. Or you could purchase the wrong member of the family fund, switch to the desired fund, and deduct the commission.

The important thing to remember is that a swap, or a sale and repurchase, should make economic sense whether it creates a loss or not. The cost incurred in a bond swap, for instance, generally should be returned in less than one year due to the extra yield of the new bond; likewise, if you've moved into a lower tax bracket (and have less of a need for the tax-free qualities of municipal bonds), your sale of a tax-free bond and purchase of a corporate instrument should result in a higher after-tax yield. Clearly, only a broad review of your tax status will tell you how best to deal with capital gains.

Charitable Deductions

Congress encourages private citizens to support their favorite charitable institutions. Many of you make such contributions as part of your personal philosophy, or your belief in community responsibility, or as a response to social or business pressure. If you are liberal with your money, you might allocate 10 percent of your gross income to your church, college, the cancer society, and so on. If you are not, unless altered by the government, you may still contribute $75 to some organization, and that sum now can even be deducted on the "short-form" tax return (used when you don't itemize deductions). Either way, the tax benefits are significant because gifts to IRS-qualified charities or institutions are tax deductible in the year they are made.

There are as many ways to donate to charity as imagination allows. One of the simplest creative methods is to donate an appreciated asset, such as stock, and take a tax deduction on the entire amount. It's much smarter to do that than sell the stock, pay a capital gains tax, and donate the remaining proceeds.

Some donation methods are so creative that if I described them here you would probably say they must not be legal — but they are. When I tell my clients what we can do to accomplish all kinds of good things, they are frequently in awe. If you don't need current income, for example, you may be able to donate an asset to charity, take the tax deduction, yet get back your asset at a later date, either for yourself or your heirs.

Other Procedures

The key to tax savings is a general awareness of taxes and the absence of panic — in short, knowledge and foresight. When you sell your home, for example, consider the tax consequences. Your profit will escape current taxation if you use the proceeds to buy a new home, generally within two years. And up to $125,000 of the profit can be tax free if you are 55 or older. If it looks like you must sell your house at a loss, renting the property for a reasonable period of time before the sale can convert your selling loss into a deductible capital loss.

Don't forget that the form in which you do business can also have important tax consequences. Partners of sole proprietors aren't eligible for all the valuable fringe benefits available to stockholder-employees. And if you do business as a corporation, it's smart to compare the advantages of sheltering income at lower corporate rates with the possible advantages of having the corporation's income taxed directly to the shareholders.

Averaging your income can reduce taxes if your income is unusually high in a particular year. If you have a large capital gain this year, for example, you may be able to spread the gain over several previous years through an installment sale. That will keep the applicable tax rate as low as possible.

In the income tax deductions department you have a lot of potential savings. You can count on at least one of the following: interest, casualty losses, state and local tax deductions, "zero bracket amounts" — the built-in deductions already figured into the year's tax tables — and ordinary and necessary expenses connected with making a living.

Exemptions are another form of deduction, a people deduction. Currently, you can reduce your taxable income by $1,040 if you provide more than half of the support of an individual who is then considered a dependent (there are proposals to increase that figure). Dogs, cats, and goldfish, by the way, don't count.

What do you know — I've spent all this time discussing tax savings without discussing a single tax shelter. Though I've touched on tax-saving techniques that involve dividing, deducting, deferring, and eliminating, I haven't even gotten to discounting and conversion. At least by now I'm sure you have the idea down pat: there are many, many ways to reduce your taxes that involve far, far less risk than the classic tax shelter. All you have to do is ask about them.

If you don't know the leading questions to ask, keep a file of the tax reduction methods you read or hear about. When examples that appeal to you show up in the *Wall Street Journal*, *USA Today*, *New York Times*, your local paper, *Money*, *Forbes*, or a radio or TV program, write them down and file them. When asking your financial advisor about tax planning, bring your file with you and take it out. He or she may be overwhelmed at first, but you will be respected as never before.

TAX SHELTER BASICS

A good tax shelter simply allows you to use dollars that would otherwise be paid out as taxes (along with some out-of-pocket dollars) to acquire assets that will increase your net worth. Tax shelters are more risky and illiquid, of course, than traditional investments such as stocks and bonds. The tax write-off, however, means the government shares some of the risk. If you are in the 50 percent federal tax bracket, you can make tax-oriented investments with half the risk, since 50 percent of the funds you're investing would otherwise have gone to the IRS. For example, if you invest $25,000 in a tax shelter in which 100 percent of the investment is tax deductible, you would have a write-off of $25,000. At the 50 percent federal tax rate, 50 percent of the $25,000 deduction, or $12,500 is deducted, and the remaining $12,500 is your own money, which is "at risk." Even a 35 percent federal tax bracket means the government shares one-third of the risk. However, the higher the tax bracket, the greater the benefit from a tax shelter.

Many tax shelters have advantages beyond the first-year write-off noted above. In some cases the investment will provide tax deductions for a number of years, while in others, the cash you receive is sheltered. These additional benefits — or lack of them — should also be taken into account when you consider tax-sheltered investments.

Another element you'll have to consider is the financial effect of the Tax Equity and Fiscal Responsibility Act, or TEFRA, passed in August 1982. TEFRA created a new "alternative minimum tax" that increases the likelihood that taxpayers will pay at least some taxes no matter how many tax-sheltered investments they make.

TEFRA did this by establishing a flat tax of 20 percent on a certain kind of "alternative minimum taxable income." You can make all the tax-sheltered investments you like, but if you fail to account for the effect of the alternative minimum tax on your overall income, you may receive only a 20 percent federal tax "savings" from these investments — and, in some instances, zero. The negative impact of this tax can also be quite subtle, so you or your advisor will have to watch for it carefully each year. In general, the alternative minimum tax can be a problem in years when your losses from tax shelters are very high or when you have large capital gains.

The biggest difficulty in shopping for a tax shelter is getting over the assumption that its tax aspects are more important than its investment aspects. Certain risky investments are given tax advantages by the federal government to encourage the public to put their money into investments that contribute to the national welfare, such as drilling for oil. Instead of funding desired programs or businesses with federal aid, the government lets citizens fund them directly. Even though your primary motivation might be to achieve a tax loss, a shelter should nonetheless be an investment, and it can be a very good investment, provided it embraces something the IRS calls "economic reality." If the IRS determines that a shelter makes economic sense only as a scheme to avoid taxes, it can declare the project devoid of economic reality, disallow all your deductions, and what's more, stick you with penalties. If saving taxes is your *only* goal, you'd be better off donating your money to charity or paying your tax advisor's bill. *Good* tax shelters, by contrast, give you favorable income tax treatment, provide generous deductions against your taxable income, a definite chance of economic gain, and a way to further diversify your assets.

There are a number of things to keep in mind when shopping for a tax shelter. The cardinal rule, of course, if it is at all possible, is *not* to shop at the end of the year: the later you do your tax planning and investing, the narrower — and riskier — the selection from which to choose. As always, the last-minute design of a financial/tax road map is fraught with the temptation to move capital in the wrong direction for the wrong reason. There must be potential economic profit as well as tax benefits, and in December, the odds are often against attractive economics. You must promise yourself to resist the December urge for tax deductions if you are not willing to investigate tax shelters for the coming year.

TYPES OF TAX SHELTERS

If you are convinced that you need tax shelters to protect a high income, one of the first things you should think about is your tax shelter mix. Depending on what you want to achieve, your shelter investments will emphasize high write-offs in early years or continuing write-offs over a longer period. You should review your needs on a year-by-year basis to determine what they really are, as formulated from your understanding of your anticipated income (for this and future years), your available cash, and your risk tolerance.

I strongly recommend you first consider the more traditional, more quality-oriented tax shelters — those with clear-cut tax advantages and sound economics. My three favorite shelter recommendations include real estate, oil and gas drilling, and equipment leasing.

Real Estate

Real estate shelters rank first among public and private syndicated offerings. More than 70 percent of all publicly owned partnerships are in real estate.

There are several reasons for the popularity of syndicated real estate offerings. The generous tax deduction per dollar is, of course, a major incentive, but there's more. Real estate is also tangible and understandable; it can be leveraged, meaning that you can get more bang for the buck; it has performed very well in the past; it can provide current income; and it is widely available, with at least five times more real estate partnerships today than there were just three years ago. Perhaps best of all, real estate still remains the most sacred government cow — even the 1984 tax law changes barely touched the best tax advantages of real estate.

You're undoubtedly wondering what sort of advantages you can get. Well, if you've invested in a moderately leveraged real estate syndication, you can expect a write-off of 20 to 25 percent per year for four years, with tax-sheltered income commencing the fifth year. (The amount of the first-year write-off depends on how many months remain in the year. If your investment was made in June, your write-off is likely to be half the annual amount — 10 to 12 percent.) As for investment quality, I'll just say that well-managed, appreciation-oriented, publicly registered real estate limited partnerships (for example) have been superior investment vehicles during the past decade. A recent study concluded that the average real estate limited partnership formed between 1971 and 1978 provided an *aftertax* compound annual rate of return of more than 10 percent. That's 2 percent above the overall inflation rate from 1971 to 1982, and that kind of showing should fit into many of your financial plans.

Locating a good real estate syndication is not an easy task. The prospectus isn't always (or even frequently) very helpful: it's wonderful that the government insists on full disclosure, but not so wonderful that the document is crammed with legalese. If you read and understand the entire prospectus, more power to you, but frankly I don't know too many people who do, including most financial advisors (who really should). Readable prospectus or no, you still need to make a choice, and I suggest the best way to start is by getting answers, with the aid of your financial or tax advisor, to these questions:

1. Who is the general partner? What is his or her expertise, experience, and reputation in partnership programs?

2. How big is the sponsoring company? What are its financial resources, and what is its track record?

3. How much at risk are the general partner's own funds? What costs are being absorbed by the general partner?

4.   How do the front-end, middle, and back-end fees compare to industry averages? (In general, look for lowest loads. In real estate, front-end fees should be under 20 percent; middle fees 4 to 6 percent for property management; and back-end fees should be payable only after you have received your original investment plus at least a 6 percent annual return. Also, be aware that no-load real estate syndication funds mean no sales commission, not no fees. The sponsors do take healthy up-front fees, and various other fees.)

5.   What are the tax risks?

6.   Is the deal compatible with your overall financial goals and your ability and desire to take risks? You'll want to go over with your advisors the allocation of profits and losses, the conflicts-of- interest, and tax benefit elements of the investment.

There is more, of course, but if this sort of close analysis is not your cup of tea, you could start your investigation from a different angle — with still another shopping list. This list, however, is a simple one, consisting only of the names of reputable partnership names you've run across. Armed with these names, you can query your advisor for his or her advice — that's what advisors are for. But be sure to pay them for their time. Insist upon it. They will have less conflict of interest and do a better job if you do. My "sure-fire" guide (in chapter 14) to selecting financial professionals, I might add, can also help you find reputable partnership names.

Oil and Gas

Though real estate limited partnerships formed in the 1970s have provided fine tax benefits, they have achieved investment goals primarily through appreciation of equity. Oil and gas investments, surprisingly, have not, despite the fact that the price of oil and gas today is much higher than it was 10 years ago. The cruel reality is that most drilling fund shelters have not made economic sense.

According to recent research in the area, even many investments made today aren't likely to return the amount initially put in. For programs formed since 1979, the odds are even worse — 42 percent will fail to return investor capital. Overall cash distributions have averaged

7 percent per year, a figure that covers both exploratory drilling (prospecting in untried areas) and development (drilling in fields or formations already producing oil). Even in less risky development drilling programs, where the success rate is usually 80 to 90 percent, annual cash distributions average only 10 percent. What's more, it has usually taken more than seven years for the cash returned to equal the initial investment. Add to these depressing figures the fact that oil and gas prices have gone down, the world is awash in crude, and recent tax law changes supposedly curb tax provisions that encourage drilling. Your only logical reaction must be to stay away!

But wait a moment. You'll recall that I included oil and gas investments as one of my anointed "traditional" shelters. Why? Just because of the deduction? No. Because good programs do work. The problem, as always, comes down to finding the right sponsor. Almost 60 percent of the sponsors do have at least one program with a total expected return exceeding $5 per dollar invested.

In chapter 12, I noted that right now may be the best time to get into oil and gas. Drilling costs have dropped 30 to 50 percent from their 1981 peak, and drilling activity is also down. Furthermore, domestic oil and gas resources are declining while we continue to import at very high levels. A recent Conoco study predicted significant increases in U.S. oil imports, from 4.5 million barrels a day in 1984 to as much as 7.5 million barrels a day in the year 2000. Some analysts believe oil prices will drop further, but that isn't so important to profitability as the difference between the producing cost and the selling price. I sincerely believe the stage is being set for an oil and gas shortage, which again means higher prices.

When you first start looking into this area, I recommend you seek out only oil and gas development programs. Since your initial tax deduction can be the same for both types of drilling, I would rather you have a reasonable chance for some success than a high probability of no success. And a good development program will return your original investment in 3 to 5 years and continue to pay for up to 20 years. Exploratory wells might be worthwhile, but the programs must be diversified and you must be able to continue to invest over several years. Proposed or even nonproposed future tax changes make an investment commitment to the longer time period very uncertain.

Drilling deals, despite recent tax-law changes, still offer some of the best shelters around. In my opinion, the initial write-off with 1985 tax brackets makes the risk of drilling most attractive. Depending on the time of year you invest, you will usually be able to write off from 50 to 90 percent of your initial investment. And a certain portion of product sales — 20 percent of gross production or 15 percent of net — might also be exempt from taxation.

Yet another reason for investing in drilling programs is the proposed changes in tax law. It is likely that your future income from the wells will be less heavily taxed than is currently the case. So if you invest before any change in the tax law takes place, you may well be improving your benefits at both ends of the deal. You will have a full tax deduction now, while your bracket is higher and income later when your bracket is lower.

How do you find the best drillers? Essentially, follow my real estate advice in this chapter, with the exception of the specific fee schedule. Also add "early cash flow" to the list.

Equipment Leasing

I believe that 85 percent of the people who purchase tax shelters don't understand what they're getting into. This is particularly true of equipment leasing programs. If it weren't for the up-front benefits, most of you wouldn't even *consider* this kind of offering. But you do consider, and you do buy: equipment leasing partnership volume jumped 20 percent from 1983 to 1984.

You're hoping, of course, to avoid paying the tax man forever. In reality, however, even the best tax shelters are nothing more than tax deferrals. The only way to escape taxes is to die . . . and some choice that is. Equipment leasing can be one of the most confusing of all tax shelters, but its benefits can be stated clearly: though it can and should certainly make economic sense, especially in the low or unleveraged partnerships, it can also be one of the purest tax deferral vehicles you can get.

Leasing involves all kinds of equipment. Limited partnerships purchase industrial, commercial, and even consumer equipment, mostly for lease to other businesses. These users prefer leasing to buying because it allows them to conserve their working capital, deduct rental payments, and avoid obsolescence. When the shelter's tax benefits are used up, the equipment is usually sold and the partnership liquidated, though some partnerships reinvest funds in new equipment. The investor's tax deductions come from the short-term (usually five years) depreciation schedule, loan interest and partnership or trust expenses, and occasionally (while it's available) an investment tax credit offered by the government to encourage the purchase of certain new equipment.

Leveraged equipment leasing plans provide large initial write-offs and an additional write-off for the first three or four years. Then a special problem occurs with medium to highly leveraged shelters: something called phantom income — that is, taxable income reportable by the investor but without any cash flow to the investor with which to pay the tax. However, as with oil, since tax rates may be reduced, you are urged to take high tax deductions now to offset income otherwise taxed at a 50 percent rate, while phantom income (when recognized in later years) would be taxed at the lower future rate.

As you can see, equipment leasing can be complicated. Once you understand the risks, you don't have to understand *all* the details — which I won't get into — to appreciate the benefit. Suffice to say that the figures are difficult to get a handle on, but one of the figures you need to pay attention to is the projected after-tax rate of return, which can reach 20 percent and sometimes more. Be sure to discuss the deal with your professional financial advisor.

Other Shelters

In addition to the tax shelters discussed above, there are many others: movie and book limited partnerships, windmills, horse breeding, horse racing, agriculture, cattle, and even more esoteric programs. In general, however, they are even riskier than the more traditional tax shelters I've just discussed. Some of the more unusual shelters, too, have abused tax laws in the past and so are more likely to come under scrutiny by the IRS.

If you require a tax shelter, most of you should choose a traditional shelter, one that matches your current financial needs, goals, and abilities. But don't forget to consider the long-term consequences as well: while a shelter may solve today's tax problem, it may also create another problem in the future. Invest in a shelter that does what it needs to do, for this year, but doesn't lock you into future money decisions that are beyond your means. And if a shelter seems too good to be true, remember the IRS's view of "economic reality."

THE WINDS OF TAX REFORM

No chapter on tax shelters would be complete without a discussion of tax reform. Tax planning has rarely been more difficult than it is now. Not only must you deal with existing law, specifically for this year's taxes, but you must also keep an eye on pending proposals — from overhauls that eliminate tax breaks, to those that slash tax rates, to those that do nothing at all.

The concept of a flat tax (or flatter or simpler or fair tax) has been around for some time. Such a proposal in 1976 was described in a San Francisco newspaper: "The bill requires, effective with the 1976 tax return, that the 12 optional tables, which cover 12 pages in present tax instructions, be revised to cover only 2 pages. The net effect of the changes will be to allow 90 percent of all taxpayers to use the shortened, revised table." That same year *Business Week* said, "Experts candidly admit that the shelter business has suffered a dire blow. The advantages will be minimized so that the shelters may dry up."

Tax reform, like the legislative process, is a long and complicated game. Many of the proposals now being considered — certainly the one put forth by the Treasury Department, President Reagan, and others — would, if enacted, drastically restructure the Internal Revenue Code. That is very important to understand. But history shows that we don't tend to change important things very quickly, especially when we don't know what the result is likely to be.

Investors are apprehensive, and unfortunately, that apprehension has often taken a do-nothing form. That, in my opinion, is a mistake. Today's tax environment is a known quantity, as is your current tax problem; tomorrow has too many "ifs" and "maybes." If those ifs and maybes come to pass, you will have to and will be able to deal with them if you have a financial plan.

Recently, an acquaintance told me that when auto business expense rules were tightened not long ago, he felt "forced" to purchase a separate car to use only for business purposes. That way, he reasoned, the IRS couldn't possibly question what portion of his other car was used for business and what portion was used for pleasure. Now that's overreacting, especially in light of the fact that the rules have since been modified.

Tax laws and tax shelters are not all that complicated really. All this media hype about them just keeps you on the money-go-round. All you need do, truly, is what you feel comfortable with, what you would ordinarily do. If tax changes occur, there will be plenty of transition time in which to plan. Even if tax law changes have negated some of my tax-related recommendations by the time you read this book, don't worry. As long as you understand what it is you are trying to accomplish, there will always be new trees to grow in your forest. You'll still end up doing just fine.

• Chapter 14

ACTION

Financial planning is a conscious process for achieving economic objectives. It is a process, not a product, so it never ends, but it isn't very demanding, either.

In my many years as a financial planner, I have seen only one kind of financial plan that I would consider bad. The common flaw in such plans has nothing to do with the goals of their creators, or their financial status, or their intelligence; the problem is solely that the plans remained *unimplemented*, fallow, useless. The hard work was already done, but the most important step — action — had been left undone. If you remember just one thing from this book — and I hope there will be many, many things — it should be the idea that an unimplemented plan is no plan at all. If it isn't put to work , your plan is useless: a road map you won't look at, even though you may feel lost.

The biggest problem most people have with their financial planning — as with most things — is getting started. By this time, I hope you've already done something in that direction. Hopefully, you've (at the very least) had a will professionally drawn (or updated) or composed a temporary holographic will. What you need to do next is set a specific date on which to begin thinking about your life goals and how they relate to your financial goals. A good date could be the next time you write your rent check or mortgage payment, if it's within 30 days. That should give you enough time to get prepared, and the check writing will be a tangible reminder. Jot down any ideas you have about your life, your family, where you are going, and what you want: anything that will affect your future.

PUTTING IT ALL TOGETHER

1. Organize your thoughts and goals in the way you find most comfortable. Discuss them with your family and/or your significant other, think about them (and nothing else) in bed, tape them to the refrigerator, record them while you drive to work, write them backward in Esperanto. Do what it takes to dredge out your closest, your deepest, truest goals. You may find the process difficult, but it may prove to be a very liberating and exciting experience. It is extremely personal, reflecting your most basic ambitions and needs. That done, you will have the foundation on which your financial plan can be built.

2. *Think about how you'd like to achieve your goals and whether your choices reflect your personality and abilities.* A common reason that financial plans go unfulfilled is that they do not make sense for the individual, even though they may be theoretically perfect. Recognize and account for your personal strengths and limitations. In order to succeed — and in order to be personally rewarding — your plan should reflect your personality. Don't kid yourself about what you like and don't like, what you can and can't do; if you're honest and realistic about yourself, your plan's achievements will be a great source of pride as well as value.

3. *Prepare a laundry list of your investment assets and liabilities.* Add up all your investment assets and all your liabilities, and try to think of everything. What you have is your net worth, and this sum will provide you with the security-building materials you need. Look for assets that could be better invested, like the cash value from a $100,000 whole life insurance policy; look for the dollars you have available — or can make available — for investment. That's one of the kindling twigs that will help you ignite something larger.

4. *Determine how best to get from today's situation to tomorrow's goals.* Now you have a starting point — your current worth — and an end point — your goals. If you rank your personal goals by their significance and the time by which you want to achieve them, you can create a road map, a series of shorter-term goals, for your life journey. For goals that require money directly — a new car, college education, etc. — think about a diversified mix of investments that takes into account your stage of financial life. Looking at your life stage will help you determine whether you should emphasize fixed or growth assets, your need for tax-deferral and retirement planning, what your liquidity should be, and the amount of time needed to achieve your goals.

If that sounds a bit too abstract, read on. In the following pages you'll see that I've put together four possible financial strategies for four stages of life. The purpose in each is to preserve the purchasing power of your assets while keeping in mind the balance between today's needs and tomorrow's wants. Please look at these charts carefully, but with an eye to your personal, individual needs. If you are prepared to perform certain investment maneuvers of your own, you should not limit yourself to the specific investments listed for your particular age and phase.

Subject: *age 30–40, single, earns $40,000 per year, has $15,000 to invest.*

Goals: *highest priority to buy a house in 5 years and accumulate $40,000 for that purpose.*

Miscellaneous: *not sure if he or she will get married or wants to.*

Amount	Recommendations	Reasons
$2,000	Ordinary income-oriented IRA	Tax deduction (has savings of $700 per year, which can be added to mutual funds); Tax-deferred high income. Predictable results.
$3,000	Government money market fund	Safe emergency money. When combined with other liquid investments, equals 67% liquidity. Subject needs high liquidity because of unsure future plans.
$4,000	Growth mutual fund investing in both domestic and foreign stocks	Investment for capital appreciation (lower tax bracket), professional management, opportunities outside U.S., and possible further dollar decline.

Amount	Recommendations	Reasons
$5,000	Diversified public venture capital fund or aggressive growth real estate limited partnership	Can afford to take risk. Will get reasonably high first-year write-off with venture capital fund and possible high reward. Real estate offers a smaller but multiyear write-off and is an inflation hedge. Either might mature in five years.
$1,000	Mutual funds investing in gold shares	Will provide income and can act as portfolio hedge if high inflation or deflation. Use excess cash flow of $1,000 per month for additions to mutual funds and money market fund. Also periodically add to gold fund. When money market fund is of sufficient size, use for next year's IRA and purchase either the public venture capital fund or real estate fund not previously purchased; continue to alternate.

Result: *Fixed income oriented: 13%*

Growth oriented: 87%

Fully taxable: 20%

Tax advantaged: 80%

Will add: *$2,000 per year to IRA*

4,000 per year to growth fund

5,000 to syndications

1,000 to gold fund

Possible 5-year accumulation for house (accounting for inflation): $45,000

Possible 5-year net worth (excluding other investment assets): $90,000

Subject: *age 30–40, couple, family income $75,000, has $30,000 to invest.*

Goals: *maintain sufficient liquidity for potential purchase of home.*
First of two children goes to college in 5 years. Accumulate $50,000 for parents and $50,000 for children.

Amount	Recommendations	Reasons
$4,000	Income-oriented IRA	Tax deduction (tax savings of $1,700 to be given to kids, to grow in their tax bracket); tax-deferred high income; predictable results.
$6,000	Mutual fund investing in growth domestic stocks	Investment for capital appreciation (lower tax bracket), but should not be extremely aggressive; fund provides professional management.
$3,000	Mutual fund investing in growth-oriented foreign stocks	Foreign stock market outperformed domestic market past 15 years; excellent hedge against further dollar decline.
$5,000	Government money market fund	Safe emergency money. When combined with other liquid investments, equals

Amount	Recommendations	Reasons
		53% liquidity. Should still have one income if other person can't work.
$5,000	Moderately leveraged growth real estate limited partnership	Possible appreciation, inflation hedge. Should attempt to have 20–25% write-off each year with tax savings going to children; a 5- to 7-year hold.
$5,000	Developmental oil and gas drilling limited partnership	Reduction of current tax liability. A 60–90% first-year write-off, an initial income tax savings of around $2,000 should be given to kids now, to grow in their tax bracket. Oil can provide tax-advantaged cash flow and is a possible inflation hedge. Energy investment provides good diversification. Could gift the partnership (and the income) to children at a later time for college.

Amount	Recommendations	Reasons
$2,000	Mutual fund investing in gold shares	Will provide some income and can act as portfolio hedge if high inflation or deflation.

Use excess cash flow of $1,500 per month for additions to mutual funds and money market fund. Also periodically add to gold fund, but only $1,000 per year. When money market fund is of sufficient size, use for additions to IRA. Purchase either oil or real estate every other year. |

Result: *Fixed income oriented: 30%*

   Growth oriented: 70%

   Fully taxable: 17%

   Tax advantaged: 83%

Will add: *$4,000 per year to IRAs*

   5,000 every other year to real estate or oil

   8,000 per year to both funds

   1,000 per year to gold fund

Possible 5-year liquid accumulation for house and college (adjusted for inflation): $55,000

Additional sources of money for college (5 years):
Possible IRA break (after penalty): $25,000
Income from oil (in children's names): $1,500 per year
Assets in children's names due to parents' tax savings: $21,000

Possible 5-year accumulation (excluding other investment assets): $108,000

Subject: *age 41–55, couple, family income $100,000, has $60,000 to invest.*

Goals: *getting two children through college (2 years), possible job change (2 years); thinking about retirement years (later); accumulate $70,000 for remaining college expense and job change downtime; and $150,000 for retirement.*

Amount	Recommendations	Reasons
$4,000	Income-oriented IRA	Tax deduction (tax savings of $2,000 per year to go to children); deferred high income; predictable results.
$7,000	Mutual fund investing in blue-chip domestic stocks	Primarily directed toward growth but with reasonable dividend income; professional management.
$3,000	Mutual fund investing in growth-oriented foreign stocks	Will have professional management selecting stocks from foreign countries. In past 15 years foreign stock market has outperformed U.S. market. Hedge against further dollar decline.
$10,000	Government money market fund or tax-free money market fund	Whether government or tax free depends on current interest rates and tax bracket. Total liquidity now equals 60 percent.

Amount	Recommendations	Reasons
$10,000	Leveraged growth real estate limited partnership	Possible appreciation. Inflation hedge. Attempt to have 25–50% annual tax write-off. (Annual tax savings of $2,000 to go to children.) A 5- to 7-year hold.
$10,000	Developmental oil and gas drilling limited partnership	Deduction of current tax liability of 60–90% for first year ($4,000 tax savings to go to children). Lower risk drilling. Tax-advantaged cash flow. Direct energy interest. Can give to children later if desirable.
$13,000	Single premium deferred annuity	High yielding, tax-deferred interest to be used for retirement years.
$3,000	Mutual fund investing in gold shares	Will provide some income and can act as portfolio hedge against high inflation or deflation. Use excess cash flow of $2,000 per month for additions to mutual funds and

Amount	Recommendations	Reasons
		money market fund. Also add periodically to gold fund. When money market fund is sufficient size, use for additions to IRA and alternate each year between oil drilling and real estate.

Result: *Fixed income oriented: 45%*

Growth oriented: 55%

Fully taxable: 0–10%

Tax advantaged: 90–100%

Will add: *$ 4,000 per year to IRAs*

10,000 every other year to real estate or oil

9,000 per year to mutual funds

1,000 per year to gold fund

Additional sources of money for college or money needed while looking for different jobs (in 2 years):

Liquid funds $41,000
Assets in children's names due to parents' tax savings: $11,000

Income from oil in children's name: $1,000 per year
Possible break in IRA for children or job change (after penalty): $8,000

Possible 5-year net worth toward retirement (excluding other investment or retirement assets): $150,000

Subject: *age 56–65, couple, family income $125,000, has $150,000 to invest.*

Goal: *retirement in 5 years; accumulate $350,000.*

Amount	Recommendations	Reasons
$4,000	Income-oriented IRA	Tax deduction (annual tax savings of $2,000 to be invested in mutual funds); tax-deferred high income; predictable results.
$20,000	Mutual fund investing in blue-chip stocks	Professional management whose primary objective is growth with reasonable income.
$5,000	Mutual fund investing in growth-oriented foreign stocks	Can take advantage of growth-oriented foreign stock opportunities outside U.S.; increases in value if dollar declines further.
$15,000	Income oil and gas partnership	Mostly sheltered 11–14% income that can be reinvested until retirement. Will participate in an energy investment with possible appreciation.

Amount	Recommendations	Reasons
$20,000	Government money market fund or Treasury bills or tax-free money market fund	Need safety of government. Taxable or tax free depends on current interest rates and overall tax bracket. Total liquidity equals 70% depending on IRA withdrawal and once- a-year sell-back privilege of oil income fund.
$25,000	Income-oriented real estate (low leverage)	Can provide reasonably secure sheltered income (4–8%); possible annual write-off of 5%; some appreciation potential.
$35,000	Municipal bond mutual fund	Should be short to intermediate term and a fully managed portfolio; dividends can be reinvested until retirement.
$20,000	Moderately leveraged equipment leasing partnership	Could provide 50–100% first-year write-off and a deferral of income until after retirement. Current tax savings of $3,500 and future tax savings should be proportionately invested in mutual funds.

Amount	Recommendations	Reasons
$6,000	Mutual fund investing in gold shares	Will provide some income and can act as a portfolio hedge if high inflation or deflation.
		Use excess cash flow of $3,000 per month for $1,500 monthly additions to municipal bond fund and $500 to money market fund. Also add $3,000 per year to gold fund. Add $4,000 per year to IRA and alternate $5,000 per year to an oil and gas income fund and deferred annuity.

Result: *Fixed income oriented: 66%*

Growth oriented: 34%

Fully taxable: 0–13%

Tax advantaged: 87–100%

Possible 5-year accumulation toward retirement (excluding other investment or retirement assets): $380,000

If all this still proves to be a bit much for you, consult a financial advisor for assistance. See step 7.

5. *Look for gaps or weaknesses in your assets or overall financial plan.* Two of my most basic rules of financial management are protecting what you already have and keeping your investments performing ahead of inflation on an after-tax basis. Now look at what you have. Do you have a will? Do you have a college education fund for your children? Are your insurance policies up-to-date? Are you sufficiently protected, or are you perhaps wasting money through overprotection? Can refinancing make your home mortgage less costly? By looking over every financial item in your investment assets and liabilities, you'll spot the areas in which your money could be doing a better job.

6. *Plan ahead for this year's income taxes, and think about future taxes or possible tax changes down the road.* The most common way to waste money may be paying more of it in taxes than you have to. If you wait until March or April to study your taxable income from the previous year, you've already waited too long to do anything. The sooner you estimate and act on your tax bill, the better chance you'll have of lowering that bill through tax-sheltering procedures and investments, regardless of any tax law changes.

7. *Gather a network of financial professionals.* I expect that the discussion in this book should provide you with something like 70 to 75 percent of the information and inspiration you need to get off the money-go-round. For the remaining 25 to 30 percent, you will require more help than I can provide in a single short book. For openers, I suggest you consult the more detailed financial books (those that look at the trees rather than the forest) and (possibly) attend financial seminars. Both will provide more of the details and financial strategies you may still require. Now that you have read this book, you should have a firm grasp on where you are headed and how to get there. When reading other books or attending financial seminars, you will now be able to pick out the particular financial information that best applies to your situation and goals.

Many of you — probably most — will find, however, that you also will require the services of a financial professional or two. That doesn't mean, of course, that you must, or can, abdicate personal financial responsibility when you consult with professional financial advisors. And it doesn't mean you have to be rich to benefit from their advice. In fact, sound advice should more than pay for itself by pointing out opportunities. But there is a problem: the fact that you already have 8, 12,

15 different kinds of financial intermediaries. Most of them are competent, but they work your information into their structure; they don't tailor a solution to your particular situation. What you get from these professionals, consequently, is a collection of fragmented, contradictory pieces of advice. However, as you better understand yourself, you will seek and better relate to an advisor who really tries to understand your needs.

What you probably need is a qualified financial planner who will serve as an "orchestra leader." And that's not just because I am one. Your advisor's function should be to focus on all the psychological and financial factors that have an impact on your life. Through information gathered from your other advisors as well as from you, the result should be an integrated and coordinated financial plan in which no phase has been overemphasized, underrated, or omitted. But such a person is not always easy to find; the profession is not yet regulated closely, and almost anyone can claim to be one. The problem is partly one of semantics because financial planning is a profession still trying to define itself. Salespeople of all kinds call themselves financial planners and most of them use financial advice as a selling tool. The quality of their advice can vary from excellent to dismal.

So how do you locate a reliable financial planner? There's the traditional approach: Ask other professional advisors and friends to refer you to one. Or contact the following organizations for a reference: Institute of Certified Financial Planners, 3443 S. Galena, Suite 190, Denver, Colorado 80321. This organization will provide you with a statewide list of certified financial planners (graduates of the College for Financial Planning, Denver, Colorado) who participate in the ICFP's annual continuing education program.

The International Association for Financial Planning, 5775 Peachtree Dunwoody Road, Suite 120-C, Atlanta, Georgia, 30342, will give you the names of the financial planners nearest you who have met the IAFP's professional requirements and have been admitted to IAFP's Registry of Financial Planning Practitioners.

There is also the National Center for Financial Education, 2107 Van Ness Avenue, Suite 308, San Francisco, California 94109. This nonprofit group provides financial educational material as well as the names of qualified financial planners.

Many planners advertise and list their credentials in the Yellow Pages under Financial Planning. And believe it or not, that's where my "sure-fire" method for finding a good financial planner (or general partner, lawyer, doctor, etc.) begins: with the phone book. (You'll see the logic in a moment.) Call ten financial planners, asking each to recommend another financial planner, the best in your locale, aside from himself or his or her own firm, of course (within any peer group, the better people are "known"). Describe your general financial situation — your net worth, your income, and the cash you have to invest — to allow the person you've called to refer you to an appropriate planner. If the planners you call are "too busy" to answer your question, well, there's a loud message right there.

From this list of ten, call the three names that appear most often. Make appointments and meet with these financial planners face to face — that's essential. See if you get along personally, and discuss what he or she would do professionally. If the planner has any written material, try to view it before you meet so you can ask good questions and can quickly compare services and abilities.

Don't be shy with your questions; financial planning is about *your* life, after all. Ask about the planner's background. Education and experience are both important. Ask how long the planner has been counseling clients on total financial plans. Ask for credentials and references.

Tell the planner you want to talk with a client whose situations and objectives are similar to yours. He or she should be happy to give you a name or two. The planner also should be able to show you a sample financial plan for someone in circumstances similar to yours. (Actual client information, of course, is held in confidence.) How does the planner select investment solutions? Does he or she do independent analyses or depend on other companies' research?

Find out the planner's area of expertise and the breadth of his or her knowledge outside this area. Does he or she know investments, tax shelters, insurance, and tax strategies? Does he or she appear to be able to work closely with accountants, attorneys, and other professionals? How does the planner keep clients informed? How often does he or she meet with clients?

As with so many other things in life, you often get what you pay for. When you choose a financial planner, fees can range from as little as free to more than $10,000, and the money is mostly tax deductible. The financial planner who charges at the low end of the spectrum is usually attempting simply to cover costs of providing a service in the hope that the client will buy an investment package. Those who charge more are often providing a higher level of individualized service and fewer products. But in either case, you don't have to buy any product from the planner: the implementation of your plan can be done elsewhere.

8. Don't file your plan and forget about it. A financial plan is almost a living thing. It's a blueprint of your life, a very personal analysis of your heart and mind. If it doesn't grow with you, you'll make decisions based on outdated, outmoded desires and feelings. If you never sit back and think again about the major issues and goals in your life, you will never be able to see the forest for the trees. Rather than keeping up with the Joneses, you need to keep in touch with yourself.

9. Believe in yourself. Many financial barriers are self-erected. Look around you: the people who seem to have "made it" — the head of your company, the politicians who run the country, the people you read about in the newspapers or see on television — are they any smarter than you? Luckier? Better looking? Chances are they're not. The one thing that successful people seem to have in common is *confidence,* the belief that their abilities and expertise are at least as good as anyone else's. If you believe you won't succeed, you won't; if you believe you can succeed, you probably will. If you also follow a custom-tailored financial plan, you almost certainly will. By using your untapped resources, by developing good financial habits and improving old ones, you will be well on your way to gaining financial control.

10. Act now. Let me repeat: *act now.* Drop this book — on second thought, please put it back on your financial reference shelf or loan it to a friend — and think about what you want out of life. Your life is indeed what you make of it; you make the ultimate decisions about its direction. You can't avoid life; you don't want to avoid life; so why not enjoy it as best you can? That means achieving goals, and the best way to achieve goals is to map out an efficient, comfortable path. The sooner you get going, the sooner you'll get where you want to be — financially independent, your mind at peace, enjoying your life and the satisfaction and happiness it brings.

At the beginning of this book I said that financial planning was nothing less than life planning. I'm sure that some of you were skeptical, but by now I hope you see what I mean. Your finances, though probably not the most important thing in your life, affect your life in untold ways, and those effects can be turned to your advantage. Gaining control of your finances, consequently, can often help you gain control of your life, and that, in this day and age, is nothing to sneeze at.

The self-control you gain through financial planning is one of the most important and significant things you can give yourself. It's something no one can take away from you. In fact it *is* you, the real you, the you within. At this point, it's up to you to decide or discover what you want from life and act accordingly. Your future is in your own hands. You have the will, and now the road map, with which to get off — and stay off — the money-go-round.

THE FINANCIAL DESK BOOK: Your Complete Guide to Financial Planning, Investments, Taxation, and Estate Planning

For the first time, all the facts, formulas, and statistics needed by serious investors and financial professionals can be at your fingertips. Authoritative, convenient, and comprehensive, this handy volume includes:

- long-term performance data of economic indicators and investments
- summaries of major tax legislation
- Social Security information and guidelines
- a primer on personal financial planning
- special sections on investment, analysis, insurance, estate planning, and retirement planning
- financial formulas, calculations, and tables

The *only* work of its kind, **The Financial Desk Book** is a standard reference volume for investors, financial planners, insurance agents, stockbrokers, investment advisors, money managers, business writers, and professional and graduate students in business, finance, and allied fields.

Over 800 Pages
More than 200 charts, graphs, and tables
Fully indexed with glossary
Hardbound, $59.95

TACTICAL INVESTING: *Strategies for Getting the Most Out of Your Money,* by Daniel A. Blumberg

By the author of *Tactical Economics*, who has twenty years of experience as a highly successful entrepreneur in the financial services industry, this book offers more straight-shooting, hard-hitting advice on making sound investment and tax-planning decisions. Blumberg applies his financial savvy to making use of economic predictions; maximizing real estate investments; new opportunities in American businesses; stock market strategies; when to invest in mutual funds, unit trusts or bonds; investment taxation; using contrarian techniques profitably; predicting interest rates; and more.

Tables, graphs, investment glossary, indexed.
256 Pages, Hardbound, $16.95

THE REAL ESTATE INVESTMENT POCKET GUIDE
by Alan J. Parisse and Richard G. Wollack

Brief and clear descriptions of key points about real estate investing are offered in this profusely illustrated, easy-to-understand laymen's guide. Depreciation, recapture, deductibility, amortization, numerous other concepts are covered in a Q & A format.

Illustrations, graphs, charts, indexed glossary,
evaluation checklist.
Quality Paperback, 86 Pages, $7.95.

THE OIL AND GAS INVESTMENT POCKET GUIDE
by the editors of CCCG.

An outstanding introduction to the basics of oil and gas investing, this easy-to-read book explains key concepts of oil and gas by means of simple examples, numerous illustrations, and clear and concise discussion in a Q & A format of risk factors, taxation and a variety of oil and gas investment alternatives.

Illustrations, graphs, charts, indexed glossary, evaluation checklist.
Quality Paperback, 96 Pages, $7.95.